Executive's
Guide to
Solvency II

WILEY & SAS BUSINESS SERIES

The Wiley & SAS Business Series presents books that help senior-level managers with their critical management decisions.

Titles in the Wiley and SAS Business Series include:

For more information on any of the above titles, please visit www.wiley.com.

Executive's Guide to Solvency II

David Buckham
Jason Wahl
Stuart Rose

WILEY

John Wiley & Sons, Inc.

Published by John Wiley & Sons, Inc., Hoboken, New Jersey.
Published simultaneously in Canada.

For general information on our other products and services or for technical support, please contact our Customer Care Department within the United States at (800) 762-2974, outside the United States at (317) 572-3993 or fax (317) 572-4002.

Wiley also publishes its books in a variety of electronic formats. Some content that appears in print may not be available in electronic books. For more information about Wiley products, visit our web site at www.wiley.com.

Library of Congress Cataloging-in-Publication Data:
Buckham, David.
   Executive's guide to solvency II / David Buckham, Jason Wahl, Stuart Rose.
      p. cm. – (The Wiley & SAS business series)
   Includes index.
ISBN 978-0-470-54572-0 (hardback); ISBN 978-0-470-92568-3 (ebk);
ISBN 978-0-470-92569-0 (ebk); ISBN 978-0-470-92570-6 (ebk)
   1. Risk (Insurance)   2. Risk assessment.   I. Wahl, Jason.
II. Rose, Stuart.   III. Title.
   HG8054.5.B83 2010
   368–dc22

                                                              2010027044

Printed in the United States of America

10 9 8 7 6 5 4 3 2 1

Contents

Preface

Solvency II is the directive regulating capital requirements of insurance companies in the European Union (EU). The directive was issued by the European Commission on July 10, 2007, and adopted by the European Parliament on April 22, 2009. It is envisioned that the directive will be implemented across the EU commencing January 1, 2013, being applicable to all insurance and reinsurance companies with turnover greater than €5 million.

The European Commission's 2007 "Solvency II Impact Assessment" estimated the initial cost to the EU insurance industry of implementing Solvency II to be between €2 billion and €3 billion. The expected economic benefits were deemed to outweigh this cost by replacing the formulaic and risk-insensitive capital requirements of Solvency I with risk-based capital requirements, improved risk management, and disclosure.

Debate continues in the prevailing mood of heightened uncertainty as to the appropriateness of financial regulation and attainability of systemic stability. After the recent financial crisis, divergent opinions are being offered on the feasibility of financial reforms and on the method and level of regulation. The principles-based nature of Solvency II represents a sea change in thinking and in logic away from some of the pitfalls of Basel II, the international regulatory framework governing banks, but reinforces the use of sophisticated mathematical methods and also the constructs of supervisory review and market discipline.

There is a danger that executives of insurance corporations will see compliance with the regulation purely as a cost and will be critical because of the financial crisis. Some outside the industry may even see it as merely the creation of a new cost and barrier to entry for other market participants, impeding a truly competitive and market-driven environment in insurance. However, these cynics are wrong. Solvency II is a well-thought-out directive, painstakingly developed over many years by collaboration between the European Commission, member states, and the insurance industry. It holds the promise of transforming the industry to a common set of standards and principles and, in so doing, creating a more stable insurance industry.

A frequent question asked is whether Solvency II would have preempted the AIG debacle of 2008. No regulatory system is foolproof, but in all likelihood, it would have done so. The holistic three-pillar risk management approach increases transparency of the level and adequacy of capital allocated to risks, and provides for an interventionary buffer between the identification of a problem and ultimate realization of a crisis.

This book explains for executives, practitioners, consultants, and others interested in the Solvency II process and its implications how to move away from cynicism by understanding how and why the directive originated, how it compares to Basel II, what its goals are, and what some of the complexities are. There is an emphasis on what in practice should be leveraged on to achieve implementation, specifically data, processes, and systems. Recognition of the close alignment demanded between actuaries, the risk department, information technology, and the business itself is stressed.

Chapter 1 explores the history of insurance in terms of the need by individuals for financial diversification, the early risk instruments and practices engendered as a result, and continues to the vital role of insurance in the economy today. Chapter 2 cites the risks to which life, non-life, and health insurers are subject.

Chapter 3 provides a chronology of the Solvency II development process, underscoring its relevance in context of the causes of insurance company failure and the inadequacy of earlier solvency rules.

The continued relevance of regulation in its current institutional genre is considered in Chapter 4. The case is made that blame for the financial crisis cannot summarily be laid at the doorstep of Basel II, and moreover that Solvency II represents a progression in economic risk-based regulation.

Chapter 5 clarifies the structure of the directive in terms of the requirements insurers should fulfill under the three pillars. The risk-based economic balance sheet approach is further elaborated in Chapter 6 by description of the quantitative requirements and their calibration under the standard formula approach.

Chapter 7 considers the techniques, challenges, and complexities of internal models. It emphasizes that the practice of internal modeling encompasses more than the technicalities of building internal models. Internal models must be embedded in the day-to-day operations of the business.

Chapter 8 focuses on the people, processes, and technology that need to be in place to successfully drive an enterprise-wide risk management project. The business benefits accruing to the successful implementation of enterprise-wide risk management is analyzed in Chapter 9.

CHAPTER 1

The Evolution of Insurance

ORIGINS OF RISK

At the dawn of modern human history, widely dispersed groups of tightly knit kin, whom we today refer to collectively as hunter-gatherers, relied almost exclusively on clan relatedness as their only bulwark against the ever-present risk of death, debilitating injury, and starvation. For these early ancestors, the concept of risk can be thought of almost exclusively in terms of the physical persons of individuals, mitigated by the guarantee of personal and kin relationships, rather than objects and possessions.

The later development of agrarian/pastoral societies necessitated almost everywhere the development of the notion of private property as the agricultural revolution made possible the storage of food and hence more complex societies. The efficiency gains accruing to these new social structures enabled specialization of labor into various trades, such as merchants, warriors, and blacksmiths, each requiring tools-of-trade assets.[1] The price of this progress was that individual self-interest was no longer so closely aligned with that of the collective.

Ever since, individuals have recognized their need to mitigate risks that have the potential for ruin, either as a result of the assets they hold or simply by the fact of their existence in this world. In other words, a means was required for individuals to achieve at least a primitive form of financial diversification. Because risk is nonfungible at the individual level but the outcome of loss is transferable in aggregate, individuals exposed to losses through common risks naturally formed themselves into groups to aggregate those risks, price the risk, and eventually even sell it to investors.

Perceptions of risk and the institutional arrangements that have developed in response closely mirror philosophical advances in society's stance on the sanctity of the persons of individuals. Risk is commonly understood to exist and require management at the level of the individual rather than the group. The market economy is the ultimate expression of this freedom to transact, preservation of which requires the existence of regulations such as Solvency II to protect individuals' rights. While it is apparent that Solvency II and similar regulations are implemented by national regulators acting as agents on behalf of an international body and bestowed on organizations across an industry, the ultimate goal of such regulations is to promote a socially optimal balance between the profit motive of organizations and individuals' rights. Article 27 of the Solvency II Directive states:

> The main objective of (re)insurance regulation and supervision is adequate policyholder protection. Other objectives such as financial stability and fair and stable markets should also be taken into account but should not undermine that main objective.[2]

EARLY RISK INSTRUMENTS

The earliest known instance of insurance dates back to the Babylonian period circa 2250 BC, when the Babylonians developed a type of loan insurance for maritime business. Examples can be found in the Code of Hammurabi.[3] Upon receipt of a loan to fund his shipment, a merchant would typically pay the lender an additional premium in exchange for the lender's guarantee to cancel the loan should the shipment be stolen or lost at sea. In effect, the lender assumed the perils of the goods in transit at a premium rate of interest. The maritime loan therefore cannot be considered a stand-alone insurance contract, although the practice proved effective enough for it to later be adopted by the Greeks, Romans, and Italian city-states. Somewhat surprisingly, codified Roman law gave no recognition of insurance as separate from the maritime loan, but the precedent of life and health insurance could be recognized in the form of organized burial societies.

Use of the maritime loan persisted until the thirteenth century in the Italian city-states of Genoa and Venice. Rigorous application of financial principles,[4] as well as the city-states' great fortune in escaping the stifling yoke of feudalism on commerce and trade and their convenient geographic location at the interstices of Eastern and Western culture, had given these merchants a commercial advantage, establishing a wealthy trading region. But maritime commerce sustaining the economies of these city-states was conducted at the mercy of natural and human hazards. Shipwreck by storm or even poor navigation was common. Ships and their cargoes were constantly in danger of being seized by pirates or corrupt officials, or made to pay exorbitant tolls for safe passage.

Nonfinancial measures were the primary mitigants of these risks, including steering clear of passages known to be dangerous—requiring collaboration, record keeping, and exchange of information—arming ships as a deterrent to pirates, and diversifying risk by splitting up a cargo among several vessels.

Financial risk diversification was already well established by this time in the form of joint stock ventures, pooling goods of a number of merchants to be sold jointly.[5] Ventures pooling goods in joint stock allowed for risk diversification at the level of the individual investor. This provided merchants the opportunity to contribute a fraction of their wealth to the equity of a venture, thereby gaining a pro rata risk-return exposure to its success. If the ship went down, the loss would be spread among a number of investors, diversifying risk at both investor and product level.

The risk diversification benefits of this arrangement were, however, limited, as the combination of market risk, peril risk (i.e., the complete loss of ship and cargo), and business risk demanded a greater than optimal degree of managerial attention from investors. Another limiting factor was that the risks were not individually hedged, but lumped together. Separating peril risk out of this risk mix lowered the cost of equity by transferring the peril risk to an external party able to bear it at a lower cost. Such specialists assumed the peril risk through the maritime loan, repayable upon the safe return of a vessel and its cargo but written off in the event of loss. The system was imperfect, however, as the debt instrument exposed the specialist to counterparty risk in addition to peril risk.

The maritime loan was thus not entirely fit for its purpose. The lender had only downside risk; with a debt instrument, there is no upside reward for the counterparty risk incurred in addition to peril risk. Borrowers, however, could only insure their venture in combination with a relatively expensive source of finance.

From about the late fourteenth century on, merchant bankers began to split the finance and insurance components by drawing up separate contracts for the debt and the marine insurance. The advent of marine insurance, the oldest of the modern lines of insurance business, thus separated credit risk from peril risk, reducing the cost of both.

This innovation spread through the Mediterranean, to the Adriatic, and the Low Countries, eventually being adopted in England some 300 years later. At the time there was growing demand to finance and insure voyages to the new colonies of the British Empire. Famously, merchants, ship owners, and underwriters would meet at Lloyd's Coffee House in London to finance these ventures. Lloyd's developed into an association of underwriters, so called because insurance policies were backed by a number of individuals, each of whom would write his name and the amount of risk he was assuming underneath the insurance proposal. The term "underwriting" is today synonymous with Lloyd's, but in fact originated in the Italian city-states.

The practice of marine insurance required Genoese and Venetian merchants to evaluate structural and contingent risks involved in maritime trade, such as the type of vessel, reputation of the captain, destination, season, cargo, piracy, corruption, and war. Although these merchants did not formalize the concept of probability in the statistical sense, they nevertheless relied on intuition, subjective experience, and objective records to guide their estimation rather than on formal probabilistic reasoning based on actuarial evidence.

Despite the lack of objective mathematical foundation, widespread markets and instruments existed for risk mitigation and risk taking by the late fifteenth century. Not only were commercially driven hedging and speculation common practice, but institutionalized gambling in the form of lotteries even became popular. Principalities found that public works projects could be financed from the proceeds of lotteries rather than by recourse to public funds. The widespread popularity of gambling stimulated an interest in probability theory among Jacob Bernoulli, Abraham de Moivre, and others. Their scientific treatment of the subject laid the foundations for the establishment of statistics as a branch of mathematics in its own right.[6] Bernoulli found estimates for binomial sums, which today are known as Bernoulli trials, while de Moivre was the first person to make the leap from the binomial to the normal distribution, typically known as the *bell curve* or *Gaussian* distribution, as a continuous exponential approximation of the binomial distribution.

More so even than fear of loss or compulsion to gamble, mortality is of course a common human preoccupation. The first example of modern life insurance was issued in January 1536 to William Gybbons of London. The policy was a one year term policy, according to which Gybbons's beneficiaries would receive £400 in the event of his death in exchange for a premium of £32. Interestingly, William Gybbons did die within the next 12 months, and his underwriters had to pay the death benefit. Given that the first mortality table would be created more than 150 years later, the underwriting of this policy was certainly akin to gambling.[7]

Insurance originally evolved as a commercial instrument, and it was not until after 1666, as a result of the Great Fire of London, that insurance for households, aptly named "Fire Insurance," emerged. The aftermath of the Great Fire saw the creation by Dr. Nicholas Bardon of the first insurance company, The Insurance Office, in 1667. To protect the houses and other buildings it was insuring, The Insurance Office formed actual firefighting teams. It issued badges known as firemarks for its insured properties; its firefighting teams extinguished fires exclusively in buildings bearing the firemarks. Other insurance companies soon followed and employed their own fire departments. Obviously this concept of each insurance company having its own fire department proved to be disastrous. Eventually a deal was worked out, and all the insurance companies agreed to donate their equipment to the city to create municipal fire departments.

Although fire insurance was initially restricted to houses, it was soon expanded to include business premises. Underwriting the risk of business premises burning down initially presented insurers with problems in assessing risk premiums, but by 1720, a group of London insurers had introduced risk classifications to make insurance available even to hazardous trades.

What happened to The Insurance Office is unknown. However, the oldest documented insurance company still in existence today began life as a fire office. Originally known as the Sun Fire Office, after many mergers and acquisitions it is now recognized as RSA, one of the largest insurers in the United Kingdom.

The development of maritime trade insurance, and later of other types of commercial and personal insurance, stimulated the creation of what we today consider pseudofinancial instruments and contracts in the diversification and mitigation of risk. Yet in the early days, the actual mathematical measurement of these risks, other than in a purely qualitative sense, was not widespread. Fine quantitative distinctions evidenced in actuarial opinions today, based on rigorous scientific method and subject to statistical scrutiny, represent a quantum leap over the rough-and-ready risk assessment techniques of yesteryear.

ROLE OF INSURANCE IN ECONOMIC GROWTH AND PROSPERITY

From its early inception as predominantly a maritime instrument until the present day, insurance has grown significantly in scope, purpose, and availability. Today the insurance industry contributes to economic growth and national prosperity in various ways. At the macro level, the industry helps strengthen the efficiency and resilience of the economy by facilitating the transfer of risk. At the micro level, it brings benefits in all areas of day-to-day life. Insurance helps individuals minimize the financial impact of unexpected and unwelcome future events, and helps them organize their businesses and their lives with greater certainty. Risk-averse individuals are able to enjoy greater utility from their most important assets via the purchase of insurance products. Almost every conceivable asset or activity can be insured through familiar product types, such as motor, travel, and home content insurance, and by business through professional and product liability insurance, cover for business interruption, and many other contingencies.

As a vital tool for the management of risk by both individuals and organizations, whether private or public, insurance plays an important role in the economic, social, and political life of all countries. Quantifying the contribution of insurance to economic growth is, however, far from simple. One such attempt was made in 1990 by J. Francois Outreville, who investigated the economic significance of insurance in developing countries. By comparing 45 developed and developing countries, he was able to show that there is a positive but nonlinear relationship between insurance premiums per capita and gross domestic product per capita, demonstrating that the development of insurance as a financial instrument clearly plays an important role in assisting a nation's economic growth.

An example of how insurance supports economic growth can be demonstrated by its impact on the private residential homes market. Without home insurance (i.e., structure and contents insurance), households would be unwilling to invest most of their wealth in a single property and would have to rent properties from commercial landlords. Hence, insurance enables members of the general public to be homeowners and supports the private housing market. It could even be argued, in fact, that insurance directly influenced the growth of democracy in the United Kingdom, since the vote was initially limited to homeowners.

Another illustration of how insurance supports risk taking and economic growth is that of the North Sea oil industry from the 1970s. The oil drilling platforms required to operate in the North Sea were not only extremely expensive to construct, but also had to work at depths and contend with conditions not previously experienced in the industry. The financial capacity of the London insurance market, and moreover its willingness to insure new and costly technologies, supported the successful development of the North Sea oil industry and the subsequent economic growth of several northern European countries.

The insurance industry also provides mechanisms that enable individuals to pool their savings to meet financial objectives, such as providing for retirement. Individuals benefit from economies of scale in accessing capital markets, reducing transaction and information costs, thereby improving the trade-off they face between risk and expected return. As a result, insurance companies are a key link in the investment chain that enables firms to finance investment and savers to smooth income over their lifetimes. The operation of the investment chain is critical to the efficient allocation of capital across the economy and therefore to improving productivity and competitiveness.

Today, in the rare instance in which commercial insurance is not available to business, alternative risk-sharing mechanisms soon arise to fill the gap. For example, in the mid-1980s, a crisis in the U.S. liability insurance market dramatically reduced the levels of cover available, particularly to large industrial companies, and a sharp increase in premium levels ensued. The response by the U.S. manufacturing industry was immediate, and new mutually owned insurance groups were quickly set up in Bermuda and other tax-haven countries to replace the missing insurance cover.

CONCLUSION

From its origins in ancient times, insurance has evolved in response to the need for individuals to mitigate against or diversify from the risks that they confront in their commercial activities, and later to guarantee their personal health and the financial well-being of their families through life and health insurance. Pooling and diversification of these risks has progressed to become a scientific discipline, in the process creating positive economic externalities at both micro and macro levels.

Today it is estimated that over 5,000 insurance and reinsurance companies operate in Europe. A well-regulated insurance industry provides economies with a reliable mechanism for pooling and transferring risk and in so doing enables greater levels of economic activity. Consumer confidence in the insurance industry is fundamental to its success. Without confidence in the ability of insurers to pay legitimate claims, the economic benefits of risk transfer would be undermined.

Insurers' Risks

INSURABLE AND UNINSURABLE EVENTS

Because the risks confronting life and non-life insurers are quantified under Solvency II with the ultimate purpose of policyholder protection, the introduction to this chapter attempts to distinguish risk from the point of view of insured and insurer. The remainder of this chapter classifies the diverse types of risk to which insurers are exposed. It is worth bearing in mind throughout this list of risk types that the Solvency II framework is principles-based, not rules-based, precisely because of the complexity of the risk landscape confronting insurers.

From the point of view of an insurer, the only constraint on underwriting a particular risk, however obscure, is that it must be able to be priced. If we are able to price risk, then we are able to insure it. Many of the risks we face as individuals are uninsurable due to fundamental uncertainty, where "uncertainty" refers to the infinite possibilities that the whims of fate and quirks of fortune may bestow.[1] The distinction between risk and uncertainty is an important one. For both insurer and insured to benefit from the contract, an insurable risk must be identified, the variability of which is quantifiable in terms of probabilities, as opposed to the uncertainty of an unquantifiable adverse event.

From the point of view of the insured, vital insurance contracts provide financial diversification from events that are likely to occur with some probability, such as a house burning down or a person dying unexpectedly, and that are also likely to prove financially ruinous if realized. In addition to diversifying from the possibility of financial ruin, many insurance contracts, such as household contents insurance, for example, satisfy individuals' risk aversion.

For the insurer to adhere to the principle of measurability, insurable risks need to be unambiguously defined with regard to a specified set of events, occurring within a specified time interval, any claim against which is constrained to a maximum specified severity, for the consideration of an up-front premium. These specifications allow the insurer to maximize the potential efficiency gains from the pooling of risk. As the number of participants in a pool increases, total risk per participant, and hence premium, decreases as risk is spread by diversification across risk objects, geographical locations, and sectors of the economy.

Efficiency is further enhanced by economies of scale as underwriting expertise becomes progressively refined by experience of claims history. From the point of view of the supply of insurance as a service, it is thus advantageous to an insurer to be large, as economies of scale yield benefits to the insurer in terms of diversification and estimation.

RISK TAXONOMY

According to the Insurer Solvency Assessment Working Party of the International Actuarial Association,[2] the five major risk types are categorized as:

1. Underwriting risk
2. Market risk
3. Credit risk
4. Operational risk
5. Liquidity risk

Barring liquidity risk, these are the risks that attract a regulatory capital charge under the Solvency II framework, whether the standardized or internal models approach is followed. The Working Party recommended in 2004 that liquidity risk be assessed separately under Pillar 2 of the framework. The five risk categories are presented separately, but it should be recognized that these risk categories do not exist independently of one another. In life products, for example, asset and liability risks are modeled together in an integrated way.

The Working Party investigated the taxonomy of risk as applicable to the Solvency framework given the experience of the insurance industry over the past several years. The document is remarkable in scope and depth but can be quite technical. Many insights have ongoing validity, referring to potential pitfalls in the modeling of risk. Perils modeled by actuaries are presented as being of necessity subject to the reflection of volatility risk, uncertainty risk, and extreme event risk in the modeling tools.

These pitfalls in the modeling of risk more generally have been borne out by the banking and credit crisis. Market events of 2008 onward have highlighted the importance of giving due regard to the possibility of negative outcomes occurring far more frequently than normal distributions or standard models would suggest. In particular, the rational expectations and efficient markets hypothesis tenets of the Chicago School have been criticized.[3]

UNDERWRITING RISK

All insurance contracts have in common the underwriting of a risk with uncertain realization in return for a premium. If the coverage of similar risk types can be homogenized by means of standardized contracts, underwriting results can be made more predictable. Claims volumes are the product of the frequency or probability of claims event occurrence and the severity of a claim, given that an event has occurred. The resulting total claims distribution may be more or less uncertain across a spectrum ranging from unpredictable low-frequency/high-severity events such as earthquakes, to high-frequency/low-severity risks such as auto insurance, which are predictable to a relatively high confidence interval.

The first consideration to be made in the minimization of under-writing risks, and hence of potential financial loss, is the criteria by which the risks to be insured are selected and approved. Accepted insurance contracts should be priced with sufficient comfort to support the potential obligations arising from them. Selection and pricing risk can be mitigated significantly through close attention to product design to preclude unanticipated risk exposures under the terms of insurance contracts.

Insurance risk or underwriting risk is thus the risk of actual claims payments, including the expenses associated with those claims, deviating from expected claims. Underwriting risk stems both from the specific type of peril covered (e.g., fire or theft) and the underwriting process itself.[4]

For the purposes of this book, a distinction will be drawn between life, non-life, and health insurance. Risk typology differs between life, non-life, and health insurance, given the nature and horizon of risks underwritten on the life of individuals, or their health, as opposed to risks underwritten on objects, possessions, personal liability, or short-term insurance more generally. Underwriting risk for life insurance includes the total of lapse risk, biometric risks (those risks attached to the health or otherwise of policyholders), expense risk for claims, revision risk, and catastrophe risk. Underwriting risk for non-life insurance includes the total for claims risk, consisting of premium and reserve risk, and expense risk for claims. Health risks may contain underwriting features of either life or non-life insurance.

Life Risk

Life insurance claims are contingent upon the death or longevity of persons. Life insurance products pledge life and/or death coverage of the insured life in the form of a single lump-sum payment, multiple payments, or regular annuity payments to a beneficiary. Life risk can be thought of as any risk contingent upon human life conditions, whether the risk of early death (mortality), the risk of living too long (longevity), or the risk of disability through incapacity, injury, or illness (morbidity).

Products that insure a beneficiary against the risk of death of the insured life within the policy term are commonly known as traditional life insurance policies, whereas products providing coverage against longevity include pensions, annuities, and endowments. At a high level, life insurance products can be fundamentally categorized as either term life products, which pay a face value upon death, or savings-based life products, which may include minimum return investment guarantees. Naturally, these products with embedded investment guarantees create additional risk for the insurer. An annuity is a series of payments, either for a fixed term or until the beneficiary's death. Endowments pay benefits on death of the insured during the policy term, or at policy term if the insured survives.

Mortality risk, longevity risk, and morbidity risk arise as a result of any uncertainty in biometric trends and parameters that may lead to an increase in technical provisions. Lapse risk comprises changes in the rate of policy lapses, terminations, settlements, and surrender. Lapse risk arises through the potential adverse effect on liabilities of early settlement of contracts or termination of contracts with surrender value, which may be particularly problematic in times of recession.

Life catastrophe risks stem from extreme events such as pandemics. Revision and expense risks arise out of the underwriting process. Revision risk is that of unanticipated adjustments to annuity cash flows, while expense risk is that of variation in expenses associated with the servicing of contracts. The most important risks to be managed, however, are mortality risk and market risk. Market risk is dealt with later as it is distinct from underwriting risk.

At inception of the life insurance contract, the insurer assumes the risk of the insured dying too soon or dying later than would be expected on the basis of actuarial mortality tables. Since a person may die sooner than expected or later than expected, but not both, it is possible to partially offset mortality and longevity risks within a portfolio by attracting clients with the desired attributes using product design and underwriting policy to set limits/goals for certain types of risk. In general, if the insurer writes sufficiently diversified business, these risks will offset one another. A systematic improvement in life expectancy will improve profitability in the mortality portfolio, offsetting losses in the longevity portfolio. Conversely, a sudden global flu pandemic that results in severe losses in the mortality portfolio will profit from a reduction in annuities payable in the longevity portfolio.

Current life expectancy is measured using mortality tables, which are published by government statistical agencies, or actuarial societies in some countries. Table 2.1 condenses for illustrative purposes the death rate for males and females in England and Wales in 2007, published by the United Kingdom Office of National Statistics. More granular tables are available of death rates by age, sex, and marital status, as well as death rates by age, sex, and underlying cause of death. Actuarial tables of life expectancy for specific age groups are derived from annual series of death rates. These tables provide a

Table 2.1 Death Rates per 1,000 Population: Age and Sex, 2007, England and Wales

Age	Male	Female
0	5.33	4.34
1	0.42	0.31
2	0.29	0.18
...		
30	0.91	0.40
31	0.95	0.38
32	1.07	0.48
...		
60	8.28	5.53
61	10.01	6.49
62	11.14	6.55
...		
90 and over	238.5	217.99

wealth of information on how age, sex, marital status, and lifestyle influence life expectancy. Insurers are also able to use these tables to monitor the mortality characteristics of their portfolios against the deviation of actual from expected mortality outcomes predicted by the standardized population mortality table for their geographic region.

The expected net present value of the life insurance liabilities are estimated on the basis of mortality tables. In developed countries, annual fluctuations of death rates tend to be relatively small, as life expectancy is quite stable from year to year, with a slight upward trend. Given the extremely long duration of insurance portfolios, some of which can be over 60 years, small cumulative changes in mortality rates over the life of the portfolio can have devastating consequences for economic value.

A case in point is the German annuity disaster. It was discovered in 1990 that life expectancy annuity tables contained three deficiencies:

1. Longevity trends had been underestimated.
2. The tables ignored the adverse selection effect created by the option to take a lump-sum benefit, thereby terminating the contract.
3. Maximum age attainable was capped at 100 years.

Since the entire industry was affected, the German Federal Insurance Regulator, BAV, allowed the required reserve increases to be financed out of future excess interest earnings. An insurer perpetrating such a large actuarial miscalculation in isolation would likely have to raise capital or be taken into administration.

The annuity disaster highlights the systematic trend risk to which mortality risk is subject. The trend risk can be decomposed into model risk and parameter risk. Model risk resulted from maximum age attainable being capped at 100, making the probability distribution of life expectancy incorrect. Parameter risk resulted from the growth rate of life expectancy being underestimated. Mortality risk is also subject to fluctuations in the volatility of mortality experience from period to period and catastrophe risk from epidemics and natural or man-made disasters.

Also highlighted by the example is the extreme nature of market risk with which life insurers are confronted. Lifelong annuities in particular can pose a great danger to the solvency of an insurer because the technical liabilities are in the form of guaranteed obligations over an extended time period, potentially as long as 70 years. No other financial system participants, not even sovereigns, are willing to assume a liability over such a long horizon. There is thus no way to match the duration of assets and liabilities. Market risk on such a portfolio can be managed in part through conservative interest rate assumptions, but this assumption relies in turn on the assumption that price stability will remain a feature of our economic future.

Non-Life Risk

Non-life insurance is variously known as property and liability insurance, property and casualty insurance, and general insurance. Innumerable risk types are covered by non-life insurance carriers. Some of the more important categories are: motor vehicle; homeowners; fire; marine, aviation, and transportation; freight; financial loss; credit loss; general liability; and accident and sickness. In the context of Solvency II, the term *non-life* is commonly used.

Whereas the amounts of life insurance benefits are contractually determined, non-life insurance claims are dependent on the extent or severity of the loss incurred. Because of this, non-life insurance policies need to be highly specific as to the precise nature of the peril covered. Insurers limit their contractual exposure via inclusion or exclusion. Inclusionary policies cover only specifically named loss events; hence they are known as named-peril policies. Exclusionary policies cover all risks except those specifically excluded by the contract; hence they are known as all-risks policies.

The key risk to be managed by a non-life insurer is that actual claims volumes experienced are more and/or larger than expected. If claims occur more frequently than expected or are more severe than expected, additional technical provisions will have to be created. Premium risk, reserve risk, and catastrophe risk may all result in the creation of additional technical provisions and deterioration of the capital position.

Premium risk arises in the event that claims in the current year are more frequent and/or more severe than expected. Premium risk is estimated using probability distributions of historical frequency and severity loss data. Separate distributions are sometimes estimated for small and large claims to improve the accuracy of the fitted distributions. The product of these frequency and severity distributions gives the loss distribution per loss event type. The normal distribution is not much used as it fails to capture the timing and size of claims. The probability of there not being a claim on any particular policy is quite high, but given that a claim has been made, there is a small probability that the claim will be enormous. For this reason, the frequency of claims is usually estimated using a Poisson or negative binomial distribution, and claim severity is usually estimated using a log-normal or gamma distribution.

Reserve risk is the risk that additional technical provisions may have to be raised against previous years' claims. At the end of the year, a specific provision called the *incurred-but-not-reported* provision is raised against claims that have been incurred on events that have already occurred but have not yet been reported. Such *long-tail* claims are an important feature of liability insurance, where claims can be presented to the insurance company many years after the trigger event. Two notable examples are the claims arising from asbestosis and birth defects due to the drug thalidomide.

In order to reconcile this discrepancy between policy period and development period, with the latter being the aggregation of claims from the current and previous policy periods, actuaries use a loss triangle to estimate run-off behavior. Table 2.2 illustrates the loss triangle concept for a hypothetical portfolio commencing in 2005.

This hypothetical insurer received €180 in premium income in 2005, of which €100 was paid out in claims, while only €30 was paid out on this business in the following year. The far right column shows that total claims paid out to date on 2005 business at the end of 2009 amounts to €139. Claims paid out over the development period thus differ from claims reported. In 2006, for example, claims reported amounted to €170 as opposed to €189 actually paid out by the close of 2009. Two triangles are created to derive statistical expectations of

Table 2.2 Loss Triangle Policy/Development Period Triangle

Policy Period	Premium	Development Period 2005	2006	2007	2008	2009	Claim to date
2005	180	100	30	7	2	0	139
2006	190		140	35	9	5	189
2007	220			160	36	8	204
2008	350				230	42	272
2009	205					135	135
Total Claims Settled		100	170	202	277	190	

the best estimate loss and worst-case loss per policy period based on the observed run-off characteristic over time.

A catastrophe can be defined as a low-frequency, high-impact event causing two or more losses over a short period, usually 72 hours. Swiss Re analysis tallies 240,500 fatalities and economic losses of $269 billion through catastrophes and man-made disasters in 2008. Tropical cyclones, hurricanes, typhoons, and an earthquake claimed the majority of lives from 137 natural catastrophes and 174 man-made disasters. Insured property catastrophe losses amounted to $52.5 billion, making 2008 one of the costliest years for property insurers on record.

Catastrophe risk is essentially premium risk in the extreme. Predicting the probability of catastrophes and estimating their losses is highly complex, as these models need to incorporate demographic, meteorological, and seismological information. The extreme nature of catastrophic risk renders it infeasible for most direct insurers to manage it in isolation, hence the need for reinsurance. Loss-sharing arrangements through catastrophe coverage by reinsurers allow insurers and reinsurers to use their capital more efficiently. Swiss Re estimates that in 2005, reinsurance saved at least 12 percent of direct insurers from insolvency, based on the number of insurers that received reinsurance payments greater than 100 percent of their shareholder equity. A further 23 percent received payments greater than one-third of their equity capital. Risk transfer is discussed in more detail later.

Health Risk

Health risk can be difficult to clearly distinguish from either life or non-life insurance. It covers risks and events affecting the physical or mental integrity of the beneficiary, the provision of which by private health insurance schemes differs widely across member states due to differences in social security systems, which provide health guarantees that may be short term or long term, life or non-life in nature.

The Solvency II Directive distinguishes between health insurance legally classified under non-life activities and under life activities. Non-life activities include accident and sickness insurance and health insurance, which is provided as an alternative to social security in the German and Austrian markets. Permanent health insurance offered in Ireland and the United Kingdom is classified as life activities. This legal classification is by no means exhaustive from a risk-type differentiation point of view, however, when one considers products such as dread disease insurance and long-term care insurance. It is for this reason that the standard formula under Solvency II makes provision for a separate health insurance module to explicitly capture the specificities of health risk.

There is some basis for the legal classification, however, as the capital requirement is calculated according to whether the technical basis for the best estimate of the obligation is similar to that of life or non-life insurance. But from an underwriting point of view, health insurance is broadly differentiated between income insurance cover and medical insurance cover. The former offers protection against the loss of income as a result of accident, sickness, or disability, and the latter covers medical expenses incurred as a result of accident, sickness, or disability.

MARKET RISK

Life insurers regard market risk as their most significant risk driver; non-life insurers also consider it to be important. Increased sensitivity to market risk of life insurers stems from their need to commit funds for durations consistent with the long-term nature of their obligations. Since the actual future payout profile of underwriting liabilities is unknown, the investment portfolio can never precisely mirror the liability profile, with the result that it is subject to price volatility of financial instruments triggered by oscillations in market risk factors.

The exposure of a financial institution as a whole to market risk can be expressed in terms of a loss distribution known as the *value at risk* (VaR). VaR is defined as the worst loss that may be expected with a certain probability over a specific horizon. Its indispensability lies in the ability to collapse probable loss into a single number across divisions and portfolios via the variances of and covariances between risk factors. VaR for market risk is driven by the granular risk factors: interest rates, equity prices, currency prices, property prices, credit spread risk, and concentration risk.

Interest rates are frequently the predominant risk factors that impact the value of financial instruments of all types, affecting the value of both assets and liabilities. Interest rates are the major risk driver for bonds and other fixed income securities, but also affect the value of insurance liabilities. The risk associated with a change in capital market rates is always present, given discrepancies in the tenor and market values of assets against the profile of obligations. Life and non-life insurers may experience quite different effects from exposure to this risk at a point in time. Non-life insurers typically hold assets of a longer tenor than their liabilities; hence an increase in interest rates will tend to destroy equity value, all else being equal, because the value of assets will fall farther than the value of liabilities. Life insurers, in contrast, frequently have unmatched portfolios of long-duration liabilities. The net effect will depend on the insurer's particular product set. Fortunately, sophisticated instruments exist with which to hedge interest rate risk, such as swaps, swaptions, forward rate agreements, caps, floors, and collars.[5]

Equity, currency (foreign exchange, or FX), and property risk are the risk of a decrease in value as a result of changes in equity prices, foreign exchange rates, and property prices. Well-developed markets and sophisticated instruments exist for hedging equity and FX exposures, but due to property's heterogeneous nature in general, markets for hedging instruments remain incomplete. In many instances property risk will be regarded as unhedgeable. While the impact of equity and property risk on value is fairly straightforward, a distinction must be made between functional FX and translation FX. *Functional FX* risk occurs when liabilities and supporting assets or capital are denominated in different currencies, allowing the possibility of a deterioration of capital adequacy. *Translation FX* risk occurs when the accounts of subsidiaries denominated in other currencies are consolidated. Translation FX risk has no impact on capital adequacy as the relationship between risk and capital does not change.

Credit spread risk arises from the risk of a change in market value of bonds, structured products, or credit derivatives following a change in the spread between risk-free and credit risk-bearing investments. Credit spread risk is included under market risk, rather than credit risk, in the Solvency II framework with the reasoning that credit spreads are determined by sentiment on the capital markets rather than being reflective of the creditworthiness of an individual counterparty. This factor thus captures systematic credit risk due to market factors rather than obligor-specific idiosyncratic risk.

Concentration risk arises as a consequence of a lack of investment diversification across geographical areas or economic sectors, or even exposure to large individual investments. On the liability side, *concentration* refers to a lack of geographical, policy type, or underlying risk coverage diversification of business written.

Insurers also continually monitor developments that may impinge on the set of available investment opportunities. Some of the most important of these are:

- *Basis risk*—the chance of a change in value due to variation in the relationship between the yields on financial instruments and the value of liabilities
- *Reinvestment risk*—the risk that maturing funds cannot be reinvested at the anticipated rate
- *Off–balance-sheet risk*—the risk of a change in value of contingent assets and liabilities
- *Asset/liability management (ALM) mismatch risk*—the risk of an unexpected change in the timing and amount of asset and liability cash flows

Reinvestment risk is of particular concern to life insurers, given that the long-term nature of their liabilities may require them to consider future reinvestment rates, if a replicating portfolio of assets of sufficient duration is not available in the market.

Market risk collectively is monitored and controlled by the ALM unit. This unit formulates a strategic investment policy that articulates risk appetite, maximum mismatch, and the allocation across bonds, equities, property, alternative investments, and cash. Tactical investment policy is frequently delegated to internal asset managers with the skills to make a call on the fundamentals of an individual investment.

It is not uncommon for insurers to mismatch assets and liabilities deliberately to generate greater returns.[6] Nevertheless, a maximum permissible mismatch as constrained by the firm's risk appetite should always be adhered to. Investments and liabilities can be matched either by cash flow matching or by duration matching. Cash flow matching is often difficult to achieve in practice because underwriting risks create uncertainty in the liability profile. Duration matching identifies assets with similar interest rate sensitivity to the liabilities. A change in the interest rate therefore increases or decreases the value of both assets and liabilities equivalently.

CREDIT RISK

Insurers hold a substantial proportion of their investment portfolio in bonds. Government debts of developed countries are generally considered to be default free. Sovereign debt of emerging market countries is considered riskier, reflected in the higher yield available on these bonds. The largest portion of an insurer's bond portfolio, however, is likely to consist of corporate bonds on which the risk of default on semiannual coupons and eventual repayment of principal may be substantial. Credit risk comprises this counterparty default risk on the securities in the investment portfolio, debtors such as mortgagors, and any other counterparty to whom the insurer has an exposure in the form of derivatives or reinsurance contracts. The Comité Européen des Assurances (European insurance federation) risk mapping also includes settlement risk as a component of credit risk, defined as the risk of a change in value resulting from a time lag between the valuation and settlement of a security.

Credit risk quantifies the obligor-specific idiosyncratic risk arising from default, downgrade, or ratings migration of an issue or issuer. Should the creditworthiness of a bond issuer as assessed by a ratings agency be downgraded from, for example, an investment-grade BBB rating with a default probability of 0.29 percent to speculative grade CCC with default probability 32.25 percent,[7] the present value of the contract will be adversely affected. Such a bond would in all probability be sold, as investment mandates typically specify investment-grade bonds. Ratings migration occurs from year to year as obligors as a whole shift rating categories due to the economic cycle.

Similarly to the banking industry, expected credit risk loss on a stand-alone basis is measured as the product of the probability of default (PD), the loss given that a default has occurred (LGD), and the amount expected to be outstanding at default (EAD). The unexpected loss is based on the Merton contingent claims hypothesis, expressed by means of a formula including the same parameters but providing an estimate of the tail loss. Credit risk on a portfolio is expressed on the basis of a loss distribution analogous to the VaR of market risk, or credit VaR.

Insurers hold the bulk of their assets in publicly traded assets, whereas banks originate many of their credit assets through their lending activities. In this respect, sophisticated modeling techniques are more relevant to banks, yet many insurers do use the banking industry standard credit risk models, such as KMV, CreditRisk+, and S&P. Many insurers regard these models as too conservative, since they do not allow for future portfolio rebalancing. In any event, the majority of credit issues held by insurers typically carry a rating from the rating agencies.

Certain credit risk exposures cannot (easily) be disposed of in the market. Life insurance is often granted in conjunction with a mortgage, with the property serving as collateral. In the early 2000s, property price bubbles formed in many markets as prices grew unsustainably. Many models, including those used by the ratings agencies, assumed that property prices could only ever go up, a heroic assumption in the light of Japan's experience in the 1990s. As a result, credit risk on these portfolios was deemed to be almost nil. However, the picture changes very suddenly after a sharp correction.[8] As the value of a property falls below the outstanding mortgage amount, negative equity gives the mortgagee an incentive to default on his or her obligation. The insurer has the right to sell the property, but will realize a substantial loss in a falling market.

Another important source of credit risk exposure is reinsurance default risk. Because reinsurance default may threaten the solvency of an insurer in the event of a catastrophe, careful consideration is given to reinsurers' financial stability according to credit rating and diversification among reinsurers to establish a maximum level of coverage per reinsurer.

OPERATIONAL RISK

The notion of operational risk initially emerged within the banking industry as a catch-all concept for risks other than market and credit risk. Under Basel II, operational risk became a specific risk category against which risk-sensitive capital would be required. For both banks and insurers, *operational risk* is defined as the risk of loss resulting from inadequate or failed internal processes, people, systems, or from external events. This definition includes legal risks but excludes strategic risks, reputational risk, and business risk.

While the adoption of a formal definition has to some extent restricted and focused the concept of operational risk, by this definition it evidently remains rather broad. This poses particular challenges to its reliable quantification, not only because the paucity of internal loss data may preclude reliably estimating probability distribution functions but also because it is often difficult to accurately quantify the actual loss consequent to a specific event. A further challenge is presented by the need to distinguish operational risk events from insurance, market, and credit risks, given that operational risk losses frequently overlap other risks. It may, for example, be almost impossible in practice to distinguish between losses stemming from inadequate or failed underwriting processes as distinct from underwriting losses. Operational risk processes around derivatives trading probably require the most careful consideration, as the highly leveraged nature of these instruments can create gargantuan exposure to losses in a short space of time using little capital.

The lack of internal loss data in the insurance industry is being addressed through initiatives such as the Operational Risk Consortium (ORIC) to collect external loss data from the industry. This allows internal historical data to be supplemented by external data (such as operational risk databases) and scenario data (the subjective development of operational risk scenarios by experienced risk officers). These data sets are combined using a statistical technique called Bayesian estimation. Bayesian estimation scales the internal data distribution by the prior distribution of data (made up of the scenario data and external data) as well as the marginal density function of the internal data. This produces a posterior likelihood distribution for the internal data. In summary, the internal data set is ramped up with external and scenario data via Bayesian estimation. The product of the frequency and severity distributions modeled on these data give the loss distribution per loss event type. Aggregation of these loss distributions produces an operational risk loss distribution (OpVaR).

From a risk/reward perspective, operational risk is unlike other risks because it is not possible to increase return on equity by assuming more financial risk. Higher operational risk destroys corporate value. Good operational risk management is therefore no different from good management. It is vital to continuously update understanding of the operational risks inherent in products, business processes, and systems. Policies, processes, and procedures should be laid down as part of the risk governance framework to forestall or mitigate as necessary identified material operational risks. Operational risks identified as having the potential to disrupt business severely should have continuity plans in place, while insurance should be considered as a hedge against low-frequency, high-impact events with potentially catastrophic losses.

LIQUIDITY RISK

We most commonly visualize liquidity risk in terms of a run on the bank with a queue of depositors demanding the return of their deposits, eventually driving the bank to insolvency as it is forced to liquidate increasingly illiquid assets. But liquidity risk is of concern to all financial institutions, whether bank, insurer, pension fund, or mutual fund.

Two types of liquidity risk may be distinguished: funding liquidity risk and asset liquidity risk. Funding liquidity risk stems from the need to redeem deposits or meet claims. Asset liquidity risk arises when an asset that is sold to meet a funding requirement does not realize its expected value because the market is illiquid or distressed.

The introduction of deposit insurance has reduced the likelihood of a rational depositor panic in many parts of the world. No such comfort is available to life insurers, which, while not having depositors as such, do have policyholders who may seek the surrender value of their contracts in response to negative publicity, a credit rating down-grade, or a general deterioration in economic conditions. Instances of such liability side risk include General American Life Insurance Company, taken into administration in 1999 after a credit rating downgrade prompted surrender of contracts whose value exceeded available liquid assets, and Equitable Life, which closed to new business in 2000 after a mass surrender of policies following a House of Lords ruling on its guaranteed annuity rate policies.

Asset liquidity risk is of particular relevance to life insurers given their long investment horizons. Asset liquidity risk is the risk of not being able to transact at an assumed market price or being required to post margin or collateral. Divestment of long-term/high-value investments, such as office towers or shopping malls, may present liquidity problems if these transactions cannot be completed in the desired time frame. Market stresses can result in unanticipated margin calls on out-the-money derivatives positions. Timing discrepancies of the cash flows on derivative instruments hedging an asset can also result in margin calls, even if there are theoretical offsetting profits on the business hedged. To the extent that liquid assets are available to meet margin calls there is no problem, but this assumption may be challenged during market stresses.

Non-life insurers typically are not exposed to the asset liquidity risk of life insurers since their policies and assets are of lower duration. However, they will face liquidity strains in the event of a decline in the renewal of policies or even a decline in the sale of new policies, and critically in the occurrence of a catastrophic event.

In contrast to underwriting, market, credit, and operational risk, liquidity risk does not attract a capital charge under Pillar 1 of Solvency II, but requires risk management practice under Pillar 2. Liquidity risk is in general highly correlated to one or more of the four risk types, demanding integrated analysis of the potential impact on cash flow patterns due to changes in policyholder behavior, market conditions, and credit conditions under adverse scenarios. Liquidity risk is entirely unsuited to loss absorption via a capital cushion as it is a cash flow–based risk as opposed to a profit and loss–based risk. It is instead managed through contingency planning and risk mitigation.

RISK TRANSFER AND MITIGATION

A wide variety of instruments and techniques are available to insurers for mitigation and transfer of risks. These include reinsurance, asset and liability securitization, hedging, and product design. Risks should be retained in line with core competencies, and all other risks should be transferred or mitigated whenever developed markets exist to do so.

We have seen that the investment portfolio of an insurer is susceptible to market swings as a result of movements in interest rates, equities, and exchange rates. Particularly for life companies, investment performance has a significant impact on profitability and growth. Virtually any market risk imaginable can be hedged, either through exchange traded derivatives or custom bilaterally contracted over-the-counter instruments. Hedging is most commonly employed to offset the risks of financial guarantees on liabilities with respect to interest rates and equity values.

A derivative contract has a predefined life, price, and notional amount with respect to an underlying security. Whereas securities such as stocks and bonds are issued to raise capital for net-present-value-positive projects or acquisitions, and can thus be of mutual benefit to issuer and purchaser, derivatives simply derive their value from the underlying. Many derivatives, such as options and swaps, are zero-sum games, as the gains to one side of the contract will be offset by losses to the other side.

Warren Buffett of Berkshire Hathaway, whose holdings have included GEICO and General Re, has called derivatives "financial weapons of mass destruction."[9] Proponents of hedging argue that it is a low-cost strategy for putting a floor under the market value of assets against adverse market movements, reducing the likelihood of financial distress or insolvency, while still giving exposure to the fruits of rising markets. Hedging may also lower cash flow volatility, thereby enhancing the firm's debt capacity and liquidity position. Detractors point to the high levels of competence needed to effectively manage a derivative strategy. An inept strategy that goes wrong may lead to accusations of running the balance sheet as a hedge fund, perhaps with more detrimental consequences than the underlying risk.

Less controversially, it is common practice for insurers to manage risk using reinsurance. Reinsurers play an important role as risk mitigators within the insurance industry, assuming a portion of a risk type from insurers in exchange for a premium, or *cession*. Diversification, or *retrocession*, also occurs within the reinsurance industry. Reinsurance contracts are classified as either facultative, denoting a per-policy level reinsurance agreement, or treaty reinsurance, whereby the reinsurer assumes risk on an entire portfolio of risks, subject to the reinsurance limit. Contracts are typically structured as proportional reinsurance, giving the reinsurer a pro rata share in underwriting and premiums, or excess of loss reinsurance, which covers all losses exceeding a threshold up to a coverage limit.

Reinsurers contribute to market efficiency in three ways.

1. They assume risks transferred to them by smaller insurers that lack the scale to use alternative risk transfer (ART) methods.

2. They assume and diversify among specialized or unique risks lacking alternatives for mitigation.

3. They provide diversification to direct insurers out of catastrophe risk. In this role, reinsurance reduces volatility risk, uncertainty risk, and extreme event risk alluded to earlier.

Innovative ART instruments, such as catastrophe (cat) bonds, weather derivatives, and contingent capital, are beginning to make an appearance. The use of cat bonds in particular has become more widespread since the first transactions were concluded in the mid-1990s. Usually these are private securitization instruments whose redemption is contingent upon the issuer exceeding a certain level of catastrophic losses. Redemption may be triggered by issuer actual loss, industry loss, modeled loss according to catastrophe modeling software, or the hazard parameter appropriate to the specific peril exceeding a specific threshold. Cat bonds are popular with institutional investors because of their high yield and very low correlation with other investments.

Contingent capital is a preexisting agreement with shareholders to issue preference shares or subordinated debt in the event of a catastrophe. This method can be a more efficient source of risk transfer than reinsurance or cat bonds, as financial flexibility is created by diversifying sources of capital, and structures can be highly customized to apply to risks that are unhedgeable.

CONCLUSION

This chapter has presented a taxonomy of the various risks to which life, non-life, and health insurers are subject. At a high level these risks include underwriting risk, market risk, credit risk, and operational risk. Life underwriting risk breaks down into mortality risk, longevity risk, disability risk, lapse risk, catastrophe risk, revision risk, and expense risk. The risks confronting non-life insurers are claims risk, premium risk, and reserve risk. Health underwriting risk may have life or non-life features, depending on the nature of the contract. The relevance of market and credit risk on insurer profitability was emphasized and these risks broken down into constituents. Operational risk is a fairly recent concept, one that will be unfamiliar to many insurance practitioners, and is certain to experience further development and refinements in the future. Liquidity risk is managed under Pillar 2 of the directive rather than attracting capital under Pillar 1 but is important enough to merit inclusion with the major risk types. Almost any conceivable risk can be transferred or mitigated.

Chapter 3

Solvency II Chronology

NEED FOR INSURANCE REGULATIONS

The European insurance industry generates premium income of over €1.1 trillion, employs more than 1 million people, and invests over €6.8 trillion in the European economy annually. The stability of the insurance industry is fundamental to the economic growth of the European Union (EU). Long before the financial crisis emerged in 2008, it had been recognized that existing risk management and solvency regulations were inadequate.

The original function of insurance regulations was to promote the public welfare by ensuring fair contracts from financially strong companies and to avoid industry failure. The market failures that insurance regulations were intended to correct related to insurer insolvency and unfair treatment of the insured by insurers.

Moreover, the important role that insurance companies play in the financial system today makes it imperative that the industry should be regulated. Insurance companies are major investment institutions in their own right, especially life and annuity insurers. Insurers contribute substantially to the economy by investing in the global equity markets, by their holding particularly of long-term bonds, and by investing directly in property.

Insurance was one of the first economic sectors to be regulated. It is subject to close scrutiny by public authorities throughout the world. Regulators' long involvement in insurance is a consequence of the industry's economic and social importance. A particular characteristic of insurance is that the production cycle is inverted; that is, insurers receive a premium up front but are obliged to pay out only if the risk materializes at some future date. This is one of the main reasons why authorities need to control insurance: It exposes policyholders and beneficiaries of insurance contracts to losses in the event that an insurer goes bankrupt. As a consequence, regulations have tended to focus on measures that guarantee the solvency of insurance companies.

WHY DO INSURERS FAIL?

Fortunately, the frequency of insurer insolvency is very low. Between 1970 and 2000, there were approximately 700 failed insurance companies throughout the world. Although this may at first glance seem a great many, the number must be viewed in the context of the banking industry. The U.S. savings and loan crisis of the 1980s alone resulted in the insolvency of over 500 institutions. Low insolvency frequency has resulted in high consumer confidence in the insurance industry. A remarkable feature of these insolvency data, given the relative importance of the German insurance industry, is how few of these failures were German insurers. Various institutional features of the German insurance market may be associated with this low level of observed insolvencies. These include understated assets, little competition, a tax regime that encourages prudent reserving, and products that have exposure limits. It is, of course, infeasible to simply transplant the institutional characteristics of the German insurance industry across the world, or even across the EU.

However, no industry is immune to failure no matter what the prevailing institutional characteristics, and over the past few decades, there have been several examples of significant insurance company failure. The most comprehensive research to date into why insurance companies fail has been carried out by A.M. Best in 1999.[1] The published report was based on A.M. Best's findings as to the failure of 640 U.S. insurance companies between 1960 and 1998. Of these 640 companies, no primary cause of failure could be identified in 214 of the cases. Table 3.1 summarizes the findings.

More recently, in 2002, the Sharma Report to the European Commission identified and analyzed risks that had led to actual solvency problems or "near misses" occurring between 1996 and 2001.[2] Usefully, the report includes a discussion of the full causal risk chain from underlying causes, through proximate causes and triggers, to ultimate financial outcome and resulting policyholder harm for 21 case studies. The most interesting finding of the Sharma Report was the emergence of a chain of multiple causes from the case studies, implying that an effective supervisory system should have the capacity to deal with the full range of causes and effects of risks faced by insurers.

Table 3.1 Primary Causes of Insurer Failure

Primary Causes	Number of Companies	% of Total Identified*
Underreserving	145	34
Rapid growth (underpricing)	86	20
Alleged fraud	44	10
Investment failure	39	9
Catastrophe losses	36	8
Expansion	28	7
Impaired affiliate	26	6
Reinsurance failure	22	5
Total	426	100

* Numbers do not add to 100 due to rounding.

CAUSES OF FAILURE

Underreserving is widely recognized as the biggest single contributing factor to insurer insolvency. It could be argued that underreserving does not directly cause insolvency because it is the pricing of insurance instruments that ultimately causes the failure. However, if historic underreserving results are used by actuaries and underwriters to price new business, future underpricing results, and so forth in a continual downward spiral. Underreserving may even occur in a more deliberate fashion rather than accidentally or as a result of poor insurance practice. There is considerable pressure on insurance companies to accurately forecast loss reserves, especially in classes of business with long-tail claims, such as general liability insurance, with the result that there may be an insufficient cushion for an unforeseen level of claims.

Another major reason for insurance company failure is the inability to forecast the impact and offset the risk of catastrophes and unforeseen losses on its book of business. A catastrophe could be either a large number of claims from one event (e.g., many small property claims due to a flood) or a small number of large claims (e.g., the destruction of a large building in a fire).

Today most insurance companies use catastrophe (cat) modeling in their underwriting and rate-making processes. Cat modeling uses computer simulations based on historical data and the insurer's known distribution of insured property. The Insurance Company Failure Working Party of the Institute of Actuaries points out that application of these techniques may well have prevented the failure of St. Helen's Insurance in the United States, which stopped writing new business as a result of losses from Hurricane Betsy in 1965.[3]

Over and above catastrophic events, which can be modeled because they repeat, the profitability and solvency of insurance companies can be affected by completely unforeseen events, such as September 11 and asbestos claims. The terrorist attacks on the World Trade Center in 2001 resulted in the Taisei Marine and Fire Insurance Company of Japan having to file for bankruptcy protection.

Rapid expansion can sometimes offer another explanation for insurance company failure. This can prove to be a causal factor in subsequent insolvency if an insurance company attempts aggressive growth through underpricing procedures. In this instance, an insurer will offer unviably low premiums to attract new customers and retain existing policyholders. Rapid growth may also occur as a result of introducing new products, expanding into new territories, or mergers and acquisitions. Any of these circumstances may result in the insurer writing large volumes of unprofitable business, if it has insufficient information on the extent of expected claims and hence inadequate funds to pay outstanding claims.

Insurers who experience rapid growth through underpricing their products are also more susceptible to catastrophes and unforeseen losses, which will tend to hasten insolvency. The true risk profile of a growing book thus may be obscured by poor insurance practice or managerial incompetence, which in some instances may even be compounded by fraudulent activity. Rapid growth and expansion have been a factor in the collapse of many insurance companies, notably the Independent Insurance Company in the United Kingdom, which collapsed in 2001 after directors fraudulently withheld claims data from the insurer's actuaries by recording them separately from the main system in order to hide losses.

A related problem that an insurer may encounter is the inability of its infrastructure to cope with a rapid increase in new business. The information technology systems might not have been designed for large volumes, or there may be insufficient staff to issue policies and handle claims. These sorts of problems can hide the insurer's true scale of losses, as delays in dealing with claims mean that claims data do not reflect the insurer's true financial position. A slower development pattern may not be picked up by those responsible for claims projections, further compounding the problem by leading to underreserving.

Insurance companies that are overly reliant on reinsurance are more vulnerable to insolvencies and failure. Although only 5 percent of failures typically occur as a result of reinsurance failure, over-dependence on reinsurance could be seen as a risk indicator when analyzing insurance companies. A strategy of underwriting risks and then passing the majority of each risk on to reinsurers may work particularly well if the market is at a point in the cycle where reinsurance is cheap. The company is left with a small part of each risk and no potential for large losses. This strategy begins to fail when reinsurers begin refusing to pay or are themselves insolvent.

Nearly every example of insurance company failure is to some extent a result of incompetent management, fraudulent activities, or both. Insurance is a heavily regulated industry, and insurance companies are expected to produce numerous reports. False reporting, whether deliberate or accidental, can hide insolvency and other reasons for failure. Insurance is a prime target for fraud. It is an easy industry for a new insurance operator to enter, money is received in advance of expenses (claims), and, although regulated, it has proven to be easy to manipulate profitability.

INITIAL SOLVENCY DIRECTIVES

The foundations of the current European solvency regime were created in the 1970s. Since then there have been many changes in Europe, the insurance sector, and the financial markets. Insurance companies are offering different types of products and investing in complex financial instruments. Techniques for risk management and accounting standards have improved significantly. In 1973 the European Economic Community consisted of only 9 countries; it now has expanded to become the EU, covering 27 countries. The regulatory response to better manage this changing landscape in the European insurance industry is encapsulated in the Solvency II Directive, which will apply to all insurers conducting business in Europe, ensuring harmonization among insurance companies throughout the EU.

Solvency II is the proposed EU directive for insurance companies regarding capital requirements and related supervision. The purpose is to ensure the financial stability of insurance companies, taking into consideration insurers' assets and liabilities. This legislation will supersede existing rules and regulations by using a more sophisticated approach to determine the market value of assets required to cover the risks to which they are exposed. The rest of this chapter examines the historical underpinning of the proposed Solvency II Directive.

Drivers of Regulatory Change

Current EU insurance regulations originated with the so-called first-generation solvency directives for non-life insurance in 1973 and life insurance in 1979. Second-generation directives were introduced for non-life and life in 1988 and 1990, respectively, with the purpose of opening up the European insurance market by allowing insurers to provide services in member states without need of a licensed subsidiary. A third-generation directive in 1992 entrenched the one license principle and provided for coordination between supervisors. The financial and technological landscape has changed dramatically since these directives were created.

Over the past three decades, a host of drivers of change to insurance regulations have emerged. There is increased competition as insurance companies have expanded beyond their national borders and also a competitive challenge arising from *bancassurance,* a strategy by which banks and insurers merge to create cross-sell opportunities. Numerous advances in financial markets have occurred. Sophisticated financial instruments have been developed, and increased market integration has enhanced insurance firms' access to deep financial markets and their ability to price financial risks accurately. Improvements in risk modeling and management across financial firms have become possible through recent advances such as value-at-risk models and Monte Carlo simulation. This has begun the process of increasingly sophisticated modeling of financial risks and a trend toward enterprise risk management. Innovations in distribution mean that firms are increasingly relying on telephone and the Internet to provide services directly to consumers. There is also a trend toward joint ventures (increasingly with organizations outside the financial services sector, such as retailers) to distribute insurance products. Demographic change and the pressures on the public pension systems may lead to increased demand for insurance firms' life and pension products.

As a result of these changes, there has been a substantial shift in the risk landscape confronting insurers. The problem with the earlier directives was that the rules did not adequately take into account a number of important risks, such as asset/liability management risk, credit risk, and market risk. In addition, capital required to be held was not aligned with the risks and value associated with a specific product sold by a particular insurance company. Also, it is generally recognized that the capital requirements imposed by the early directives were too low to ensure adequate solvency of many firms. Finally, the early directives did not provide supervisors with the tools and procedures to intervene, which is arguably as important for policyholder protection as the level of solvency itself.

Although the initial directives had the advantage that they could be implemented at a relatively low cost to insurance companies, while also providing a degree of policyholder protection, they were clearly an oversimplification as they were not risk-based, falling short of delivering the desired economic benefits. Lessons learned during 2000 and 2001, when equity markets fell sharply, resulting in insurance company failures such as Equitable Life in the United Kingdom, increased industry demand for regulatory scrutiny of best risk management practice.

Nonharmonized Solvency Rules

The limitations and weaknesses of the initial solvency directives led some European countries, including the United Kingdom, Denmark, Germany, the Netherlands, and Switzerland, to introduce significant changes to the assessment of insurance solvency requirements. The remaining part of this section provides further detail around the regulations currently operating in the United Kingdom, Switzerland, and Denmark.

United Kingdom

On January 1, 2005, the United Kingdom's Financial Services Authority (FSA) introduced a new risk-based solvency capital requirement. The principles behind the FSA's prudential structure were to ensure that insurance companies are responsible for sound financial risk management and proper capital funding of assets and liabilities. There are three components to the FSA's solvency legislative framework: technical provisions and capital requirements, self-assessment of capital requirements, and supervisory review.

Technical provisions cover the realistic valuation and risk-sensitive liability obligations of insurance firms. Life insurance companies are required to calculate realistic valuations of their liabilities, which require fair valuation of discretionary benefits, guarantees, and options. Non-life insurers must calculate the enhanced capital requirement (ECR), a factor-based formula that gives different weights to assets, provisions, and premiums.

The second part of the FSA's framework is insurance companies' self-assessment of their capital needs, also known as the Individual Capital Adequacy Standards (ICAS). This standard allows insurers to use internal models to calculate their capital requirements, enabling them to move from rules-based regulation and adopt a principles-based approach. The burden now moved to the company to justify the amount of capital held, as management should be in the best position to properly understand the risks inherent in their business.

The final part of the regime is the Supervisory Review Process. The Individual Capital Guidance is the FSA's view of the required capital. If there is a significant gap between the regulator's and the insurer's view of capital, the FSA has authority to intervene.

In October 2007, the U.K. FSA published a report called "ICAS—Lessons Learned and Looking Ahead to Solvency II." This report concluded that the new requirements had encouraged a risk management culture within insurers. The investment in capital modeling was considered a success, with the majority of firms employing the models to support key decisions such as dividend payment, reinsurance purchase, and due diligence on acquisitions.

Switzerland

As a consequence of the market crash in 2001 and 2002, the Swiss insurance regulator, the Federal Office of Private Insurers (FOPI), recognized that there were inadequacies with the existing solvency regulations, particularly with respect to exposure to equity risk. To protect the industry, the FOPI began development, in close cooperation with the Swiss insurance industry, of the Swiss Solvency Test (SST). The first field test was performed in 2005; it included 15 life, 15 non-life, and 15 health insurance companies, representing approximately 90 percent of the Swiss insurance market. Further tests took place in 2006. In 2008, the SST became mandatory for all insurance and reinsurance companies domiciled in Switzerland.

The SST works by calculating two values, risk-bearing capital and target capital, and asks: "How much capital do I need at the beginning of the year in order to be able to cover the liabilities at the end of the year with a 99 percent probability?" The *risk-bearing capital* is the difference between the market-consistent value of assets less the market-consistent value of liabilities, plus the market value margin. *Target capital* is defined as the sum of the expected shortfall of change in risk-based capital, within one year at a 99 percent confidence level, plus the market value margin (MVM). The MVM, which is also called the risk margin, is discussed in more detail in Chapter 6. Under the SST, if the risk-bearing capital is greater than the target capital, then the insurer is assumed to be solvent.

There are many similarities between the SST and the proposed Solvency II Directive. The SST is based on a market-consistent valuation of the assets and liabilities. Risks taken into consideration are market, credit, and insurance risks; Solvency II also includes operational risk. Similarly to Solvency II, the Swiss regulator also offers a standard model approach; however, insurance companies are encouraged to use internal models.

Denmark

In June 2001 the Danish Financial Supervisory Authorities (DFSA) introduced a new risk-based solvency reporting system for its life and pension companies. This new system quickly became known as the traffic light system. The traffic light system is a scenario-based supervision tool that requires Danish life and pension companies to submit semiannual reports on their base capital according to adverse changes in key market variables as defined in "red light" and "yellow light" scenarios.

The yellow light scenario serves as an early warning indicator. It involves a 100 basis points (bps) decrease in interest rates, a 30 percent decline in stock prices, and a 12 percent reduction in real estate investment values. Companies that can pass this scenario without experiencing solvency problems can operate in a "green light" status. Companies whose base capital falls below the critical level in this scenario receive yellow light status and are then required to submit a more frequent (quarterly) solvency report.

The red light scenario involves a 70 bps decrease in interest rate level, a 12 percent decline in stock prices, and an 8 percent decrease in real estate investment values. This stress is much milder than under the yellow light scenario, indicating that a company incapable of passing the stress is much closer to insolvency. Companies whose base capital falls below the critical level in this scenario receive red light status and will be strictly monitored by the DFSA and required to submit a monthly solvency report.

When the traffic light system was introduced in June 2001, about 30 percent of all Danish life and pension companies were flagged as either red or yellow status. Three years later, in mid-2004, all insurers operated under a green light. The success of the Danish system led other countries to consider a similar mechanism. In January 2006, the Swedish Financial Services Authority implemented its own version of the traffic light system for Swedish life and pension companies.

Solvency I

The initial solvency directives were updated in 2002 with the creation of the Solvency I Directive. The lack of alignment between capital requirements and the risks inherent to the products offered by insurers are reflected in the simplicity of the capital requirement calculation under Solvency I.

For non-life insurance, the required solvency margin is defined as the higher of either the premium or the claims index. These indexes are calculated using these formulas:

Premium index = 18% × the first €50 million gross premiums + 16% × the remaining gross premiums

Claims index = 26% × the first €35 million gross claims + 23% × the remaining gross claims, where gross claims are averaged over the past 3 to 7 years depending on the class of business

For life insurers, the minimum solvency margin is calculated as:

Solvency margin = 4% × nonlinked reserves +
1% linked reserves + 0.3% × death strain at risk

The minimum guarantee fund, as defined by the directive, is set at one-third of the required solvency margin, subject to a minimum of €2 million to €3 million, depending on the line of business. In addition to the solvency regulations, the EU defines investment guidelines, governing how technical reserves are to be invested, by imposing restrictions on the asset classes in which insurers are allowed to invest, and the maximum percentage they are allowed to hold in each class.

Regulators and insurance and risk experts felt that Solvency I suffered severe limitations:

- It is based on simplistic formulas that create perverse incentives in capital requirements and inconsistent treatment of policyholders.

- It is an accounting approach that limits recognition of diversification and risk mitigation.

- It is a solo company regulation.

- It has limited risk governance and risk disclosure requirements.

The apparent weaknesses of the regulations prompted the European Parliament to lay out the key principles that would underpin Solvency II, such as the three-pillar structure, risk-based supervision, and fair value, concurrent with the introduction of Solvency I. In addition to being risk-based, one of the primary objectives of the Solvency II regulations is to ensure harmonization among insurance companies throughout the EU.

The remainder of this chapter covers the background and timetable for implementation of this legislation.

PROCESS OF THE SOLVENCY II PROJECT

The first phase of Solvency II occurred between spring 2001 and autumn 2003. During this phase the EU commissioned two studies to develop a high-level framework for a new solvency regime for insurance companies. The first study, the Sharma Report, was published in December 2002. This report stated that capital requirements are necessary for insurance supervision but should be seen as just one of the preventive tools requiring supervisory intervention. The second study, titled "A Global Framework for Insurer Solvency Assessment," looked at methods to assess the overall financial position of insurers. This study recommended a more risk-based approach and economic view for solvency assessment.

The conclusion from these studies was that the insurance industry should implement regulations similar to Basel II, a three-pillar structure, which combines quantitative and qualitative measures. Chapter 4 details some of the regulatory learning transfer from Basel II to Solvency II, while Chapter 5 covers the structure of the Solvency II framework in more detail.

The Solvency II project follows the Lamfalussy Process (described next), the first level of which began in 2004 and concluded in April 2009 with the adoption of the Solvency II Framework Directive by the European Parliament and Council. During the first level of the Lamfalussy Process, a formal consultation procedure was required. This consultation period involved three waves of calls for advice and a series of impact assessments. These calls for advice took place over a nine-month period in 2005 and 2006. The impact assessments, also referred to as the quantitative impact studies (QISs), began in 2005. As of July 2010, four QISs had been completed, with a fifth issued.

After the European Parliament's approval of the Level 1 Solvency II Framework Directive on April 22, 2009, the focus changed to Level 2 advice, which was duly issued by the Committee of European Insurance and Occupational Pensions Supervisors (CEIOPS) in November 2009, concurrent with the publication of the full text of the Solvency II Directive. The position of CEIOPS in respect of the EU will be covered later in the chapter. The proposed date for implementation of Solvency II is January 1, 2013, by which time all EU member states, plus Norway, Iceland, and Liechtenstein, must bring into force the laws, regulations, and administrative provisions necessary to comply with Solvency II.

Lamfalussy Process

The Lamfalussy Process is an approach for the development of financial service industry regulations used by the EU. Originally developed in March 2001, it is named after the chair of the EU advisory committee that created it, Alexandre Lamfalussy. It is composed of four levels, each focusing on a specific stage of the implementation of legislation. Table 3.2 illustrates these four levels. The Lamfalussy Process is intended to provide several benefits over traditional lawmaking, including more consistent interpretation, convergence in national supervisory practices, and a general enhancement in the quality of legislation of financial services.

Nevertheless, the process has provoked controversy as it allows some bypassing of accountable oversights by the EU Council and the elected European Parliament. In November 2007 the European Commission published a report, "Communication on the Review of

Table 3.2 Solvency II, Lamfalussy Process

	What Is It?	What Does It Include?	Who Develops It?	Who Decides?
Level 1	Solvency II Directive	Overall framework principles	European Commission	European Parliament European Council
Level 2	Implementing measures	Detailed implementation measures	European Commission	European Commission, but with consent of EIOPC and European Parliament
Level 3	Supervisory standards	Guidelines to apply in day-to-day supervision	CEIOPS	CEIOPS
Level 4	Evaluation	Monitoring compliance and enforcement	European Commission	European Commission

Source: CEA, "Solvency II: Understanding the Process," February 2007. Comité Européen des Assurances.

the Lamfalussy Process." The report found that the Lamfalussy Process provides the right framework and had met its overall objectives. However, the general consensus among financial experts was that some important changes were required in order to make it more efficient. In particular, the functioning of the Level 3 committees was highlighted as an area requiring improvement to enhance supervisory convergence and cooperation.

At the first level of the process, the European Parliament and EU Council adopt a piece of legislation (e.g., Solvency II), establishing the core values of a law and building guidelines on its implementation. The law then progresses to the second level. At Level 2, sector-specific committees and regulators advise on technical details and then bring it to a vote in front of member-state representatives. At Level 3, national regulators work on coordinating new regulations with the European Commission. The fourth and final level involves compliance and enforcement of the new rules and laws.

Stakeholders

A large number of organizations and individuals are involved in the development of the Solvency II project: the European Commission, member states through their participation in the European Insurance and Occupational Pensions Committee (EIOPC), the Committee of European Insurance and Occupational Pensions Supervisors (CEIOPS), the Groupe Consultatif Actuariel Européen, the Chief Risk Officer Forum (CRO Forum), the European insurance industry (Comité Européen des Assurances [CEA]), and the Association of Mutual Insurers and Cooperatives in Europe (AMICE). The European Parliament is also showing a great deal of interest, and several information sessions have already been organized for members of the Economic and Monetary Committee. The involvement of so many people upstream should ultimately make it easier to agree upon the new solvency rules.

CEIOPS

CEIOPS was founded on November 5, 2003, in line with the Lamfalussy Process. It is headquartered in Frankfurt, Germany, and is composed of representatives from the insurance and occupational pension supervisory authorities of the EU as well as Norway, Iceland, and Liechtenstein. The purpose of this organization is to provide advice to the European Commission on the drafting of implementation measures for legislative directives and regulations covering insurance companies and occupational pension firms. Besides issuing supervisory guidelines for the governance by the national supervisory authorities, CEIOPS is also responsible for the calls for advice and QISs that form a key input into the EU's Impact Assessment report of the Solvency II Framework Directive.

CEA

The CEA is the European insurance and reinsurance federation. Founded in 1953, its original aim was to monitor the works of the Organisation for Economic Co-operation and Development. Now the CEA, through its 33 member bodies, comprising national insurance associations, represents all types of insurance and reinsurance organizations in Europe. The purpose of the CEA is to represent all European insurers and reinsurers within the EU and other international regulatory bodies. In particular, its focus is to raise awareness of insurers' and reinsurers' roles in providing insurance protection and security to the community as well as contributing to economic growth and development. The CEA, together with the Groupe Consultatif, the association of professional actuarial bodies within the EU, has led the industry work on Solvency II. They established working groups for Solvency II that provided effective consultation with those created by CEIOPS.

EIOPC

The EIOPC is based in Brussels and was created by the EU Directive 2004/9/EC in accordance with the Lamfalussy committee structure to replace the former Insurance Committee. It assists the EU Commission in adopting and implementing measures for the EU's legislations. The committee consists of national finance ministries or their equivalent for all countries covered by the EU. In 2009, after the Solvency II framework was agreed upon, the EIOPC began preparing implementing measures, providing the detailed specifications required to apply the measures described in the directive. These are the Level 2 measures under the Lamfalussy Process.

Chief Risk Officer Forum

The CRO Forum was formed in 2004 and is comprised of senior risk officers from the largest European insurance and reinsurance companies, including Allianz, AXA, Munich Re, and Generali. The objectives of this organization are focused on developing and promoting industry best practices in risk management. The CRO Forum has been heavily involved in providing input for the Framework Directive and continues to be vocal in its support for the Solvency II Directive.

AMICE

In January 2008, Association International des Societes d'Assurances Mutuelle (AISAM) and the Association of European Cooperative and Mutual Insurers (ACME) joined to form AMICE. With over 1,700 members, AMICE represents over one-third of the insurance companies in Europe and accounts for approximately 20 percent of the premium revenue. The primary goal of this organization is to ensure that mutual and cooperative insurance companies are represented in securing a level playing field for all insurers in Europe, especially within the scope of the Solvency II Directive.

Quantitative Impact Studies

As part of the second wave of calls for advice during the Solvency II process, the European Commission requested that CEIOPS create a series of studies—the QISs—to gain insight into the quantitative impact of the new Solvency II regulations on insurance companies. The results from these QISs are to provide key input into the Solvency II Directive. As of July 2010, four QISs had been completed, with QIS 5 planned to take place during 2010. The objectives and results from each QIS are available from CEIOPS.

First Quantitative Impact Study

The first quantitative impact study was undertaken between October and December 2005. QIS 1 focused on the level of prudence in the current technical provisions, benchmarking them against predefined confidence levels. Over 300 insurers from 19 countries provided information for QIS 1, and the results were published in February 2006. The general conclusions were that the best estimate plus risk margin tended to be less than the provisions on the existing Solvency I basis and that the risk margins tend to be small for most undertakings and classes of business. These findings showed that the Solvency II proposals would have significant implications, although the total effect could be assessed only after the second quantitative impact study exercise.

Second Quantitative Impact Study

In spring 2006, CEIOPS conducted its second quantitative impact study, QIS 2. This study was broader and more comprehensive than QIS 1. Its main purpose was to test the solvency requirements proposed in the Solvency II regulations, the solvency capital requirements (SCR) and minimum capital requirements (MCR).

The results from QIS 2 were published in December 2006 and showed an increase in the number of participants from the previous study, with a total of 514 insurers providing results for QIS 2. The main issue that emerged from QIS 2 was the inconsistent relationship between the SCR and MCR calculations, which in some instances resulted in a higher MCR than SCR. As a result, the "ladder of intervention," covered in Chapter 5, which allows regulators to intervene prior to final run-off of liabilities, would not work properly.

Third Quantitative Impact Study

The third quantitative impact study took place from April to June 2007. The aim of QIS 3 was to improve the calibration of the solvency (SCR and MCR) requirements and understand the possible impact on the balance sheet of the amount of capital required for insurance companies. The total number of participants was 1,027, nearly double that of QIS 2. The general consensus was that QIS 3 was an improvement on QIS 2, but a number of areas still needed to be addressed, including:

- Further modifications to the calibration of the SCR standard approach
- Whether the calculations were too complicated for smaller insurers, especially in calculating market-consistent liabilities
- Further guidance on the cost-of-capital approach

This study also addressed the effects of Solvency II on insurance groups for the first time. Insurance groups are a collection of silo or separate insurance companies that report to a corporate insurance company. Such insurance groups have been established in the EU for a number of different reasons, including improved management accountability, cross-border activities, mergers and acquisitions, legal requirements to separate life and non-life business, and taxation implications. Unfortunately, due to a low participation rate, less than 5 percent of the insurers that supplied data were groups, so it was difficult to draw any meaningful results. The fourth quantitative impact study would place greater emphasis on insurance groups to supply information.

Fourth Quantitative Impact Study

CEIOPS conducted QIS 4 between April and July 2008, and the results were published in November 2008. Approximately one-third of all European insurers participated in QIS 4, an increase of about 40 percent from QIS 3 participation rates. Nevertheless, these insurers represented over 60 percent of the EU premium revenue market share. This participation far exceeded the expectations of the European Commission and highlighted the importance of Solvency II to the insurance industry. Like the previous studies, QIS 4 concentrated on the Pillar 1 quantitative aspects of the Solvency II Directive. Nearly 90 percent of the insurance companies were able to meet the new SCR and only a small number of insurers (17) failed to obtain the MCR.

A total of 111 insurance groups from 16 countries provided data for QIS 4, a significant improvement on QIS 3. It was hoped that a group support regime would be introduced whereby parent companies would have to commit to the transfer of capital to subsidiaries as needed. Given the calculation of a single SCR for the whole group, this would mean a smaller amount of capital allocated for the risks of the group. Many member states opposed the regime on the grounds that they would lose sovereignty as host countries. The group support regime will be revisited in 2015.

CONCLUSION

This chapter has provided a chronology of the Solvency II project process, underscoring its relevance in context of the need for regulation, the causes of insurance company failure, and the inadequacy of previous generation solvency rules. The collaborative process that has been followed between the European Commission, member states, and the insurance industry was outlined.

Given the complexity of the insurance industry, and the growth of the European Union in the last 10 years, Solvency II is probably the most ambitious financial services legislation ever implemented. It will completely change the measurement of the financial stability of European insurers and affect over 5,000 insurance companies in 30 different countries across the EU. It is expected that the legislation will also have implications throughout the world as non-European insurers implement similar solvency and risk management requirements. The complex approval process and the inevitable delays in finalizing the requirements and implementing the legislation merely serve to highlight the significance of these regulations. In addition, the high level of participation in the quantitative impact studies indicates the importance that insurers are attaching to the Solvency II Directive.

Chapter **4**

Learning from the Basel Approach

REGULATION IN THE CONTEXT OF THE CREDIT CRISIS

Following the extreme market gyrations of August 2007 through the end of 2008, the world confronted an unprecedented failure and near collapse of the entire financial system. Given that extreme, persistent write-downs on bank assets were one of the main causes of the financial crisis, a cynical observer might argue that the Basel II regulatory framework governing their conduct was an unmitigated disaster. If this is the case, what are the implications for the adoption of an industry-wide risk management standard such as Solvency II? The question as to whether regulation can prevent crises is addressed as a preamble to this chapter. Misapprehensions regarding the scope and capacity of regulation to avert crises may obfuscate recognition of the innovation and opportunity presented by a risk management framework such as Solvency II.

Write-downs of bank assets played the final act in a credit boom that fueled a bull market in stocks and a near-decade-long housing price bubble, the bursting of which in 2007 unearthed the extent of subprime mortgages and subsequently triggered the credit crisis. The crisis was popularly construed as being the result of regulatory failure, but it highlights the tendency for financial innovation to circumvent regulation. Because Basel II, the capital requirement introduced in 2005, required banks to hold expensive capital against loan defaults, banks innovated by shifting some assets off balance sheet. The techniques included securitizations of underlying assets such as subprime mortgages, structured investment vehicles, and credit default swaps insuring against borrower default. Liquidity concerns and reputational considerations stemming from the uncertainty associated with counterparty losses prompted banks to take these assets back onto their balance sheets at greatly reduced valuations, which required them to seek new capital.

The reduced valuations at which banks were required to take assets back onto their balance sheets were the subject of bankers' own objections to the regulatory framework. Banks are required to mark their assets to market quarterly under fair value reporting standards of the U.S. Financial Accounting Standards Board's (FASB) Generally Accepted Accounting Principles (GAAP) rules and the International Accounting Standards Board's (IASB) International Financial Reporting Standards (IFRS). Politicians, however, launched three related objections:

1. They condemned Basel II for incentivizing banks to hold less capital (by way of a more granular understanding of their risks).
2. They scapegoated the use of regulatory arbitrage through off-balance-sheet financing as a root cause of financial instability.
3. They questioned why banks were allowed to trade in complex structured credit products.

But politicians encouraged banks to make high-risk (subprime) loans. The U.S. Community Reinvestment Act of 1977, evolving through several subsequent legislative and regulatory changes, mandates banking institutions to meet the credit needs of borrowers in all segments of their communities. These provisions received further reinforcement with 1992 legislation requiring the government-sponsored mortgage giants, the Federal National Mortgage Association and the Federal Home Mortgage Corporation (commonly referred to as Fannie Mae and Freddie Mac, respectively) to allocate a percentage of their lending to meeting affordable housing goals. By the end of 2007, they supported a combined $5.2 trillion of debt and guarantees on capital of $83.2 billion, a gearing of 65 to 1. In September 2008, the U.S. government was forced to bail out and recapitalize both of these giants in a bid to stabilize the secondary mortgage market.

Ultimate responsibility should perhaps rest with financial executives who sanctioned the practice of bundling risky assets such as subprime mortgages into complex structured products,[1] which the ratings agencies then endorsed with their AAA ratings. The AAA stamp of approval allowed these structured products to be shifted off–balance sheet into structured investment vehicles consisting of securitizations of assets, freeing up precious bank capital for another round of asset origination and distribution. Structured products provided the bridge between bankers eager to expand their balance sheets using the low funding rates prevalent in wholesale funding markets and investors hungry for yield. Neither party gave due consideration to the inherent riskiness of this activity—after all, the paper had been stamped AAA. The greed and incompetence prevalent throughout the financial system was neatly captured in Citigroup's erstwhile chief executive officer (CEO) Chuck Prince's now infamous comment to the *Financial Times*: "As long as the music is playing, you've got to get up and dance."[2]

Perhaps the single most shocking event of the credit crisis was the $123 billion bailout of U.S.-based American International Group (AIG). AIG seemed completely ignorant of the risks associated with writing over $440 billion notional value worth of credit default swaps (CDSs). CDSs are credit derivatives insuring the purchaser against the default of a third party. Strategies such as writing CDS contracts generate a steady income over long periods of time, punctuated by occasional catastrophic losses—sometimes referred to as "picking up nickels in front of steam-rollers."[3] Complex assets and liabilities such as CDSs that are many steps removed from the underlying exposures require complex mark-to-model pricing. When market liquidity dries up, the broad assumptions underpinning such models break down. Over the credit cycle, pricing becomes volatile, prone to manipulation, and even dangerous in the context of prevailing leverage multiples.

AIG's nationalization is directly attributable to the mark-to-model write-downs on its assets reflecting increased, but probably temporary, risk and liquidity premiums. Martin Sullivan, CEO at the time, lobbied regulators to discard fair value accounting rules, proposing instead that companies estimate the maximum losses likely to be incurred over time for recognition in the income statement. The rationale for such an approach is that write-downs during times of market stress exceed actual or probable loss. While fair value accounting indisputably contributes to procyclicality in the financial system, financial reporting requires a snapshot of a company's current financial position.

Few would disagree that it is neither feasible nor even perhaps desirable to create a crisis-proof financial system. The existence of moral hazard precludes the possibility of preventing institutional bankruptcy. Eliminating boom-bust cycles is clearly impossible. But given the sheer scale of the 2008 credit crisis, the voting public is likely to seek both retribution and guarantees. The guarantees are likely to take the form of closer regulation and supervision. A more rules-based regulatory framework is neither a necessary nor a sufficient condition to ensure financial stability. The word "credit" is derived from the Latin *credere*, meaning "to trust." Relationships of trust govern the actions of individuals in every facet of life according to social and cultural norms, underpinned by societal institutions, such as regulations and bankruptcy procedures. Trust cannot be regulated.

Procyclicality and attendant periodic panic is inherent in any financial system, including Basel II or any other conceivable regulatory framework. There is a strong empirical correlation between bank profits and asset prices. During economic booms, asset prices trend upward, bad debts are low and margins strong. Profit growth lifts bank share prices, making it easy to raise capital. This process reverses during a slump. Proposals to temper Basel II's procyclicality include stronger prudential oversight of capital, liquidity, and risk management; enhanced transparency and disclosure; and changing the business model of ratings agencies and the uses of their ratings. Given the extent of the damage incurred and the staggering sums provided to the financial industry as a safety net, stricter and more intrusive regulation seems a fait accompli.

It is perhaps too convenient therefore, too obviously gratifying, to apportion blame squarely at the door of Basel II, or even risk management in general, while evidence suggests that in fact the converse is true. Many large international banks, such as London-based HSBC for example (as of 2010 the world's largest banking and financial services group), emerged relatively unscathed from the crisis as a result of embracing not just the letter but also the spirit of Basel II by not seeking out excessive regulatory arbitrage. Cushioned by low loan-to-deposit ratios, moderate off–balance-sheet financing, and little exposure to complex structured assets, HSBC's market capitalization declined just $46 billion to $169 billion between the second quarter of 2007 and third quarter of 2008. By contrast, HSBC's bigger rival Citigroup experienced a $173 billion decline to $82 billion over the same period.

The rest of this chapter provides some context to the evolution of financial regulation by briefly summarizing the political and economic origins of the Basel Accord before elaborating further on Solvency II.

EVOLUTION OF BANKING REGULATION

The 1988 Basel Accord stipulated that banks should hold regulatory capital greater than or equal to 8 percent of their risk-weighted assets. The 8 percent capital requirement represented a minimum lower regulatory bound, but more could, in principle, be demanded on an individual basis at the discretion of the various national supervisors, as dictated by circumstances.

Within a relatively short time, the application of standardized risk weightings to asset classes proved to be a key weakness of the original Basel Accord. It generated powerful incentives for regulatory arbitrage, since required regulatory capital frequently diverged markedly from the market's perception of desirable economic capital. A very common instance of such arbitrage occurred with the securitization of lending to high-quality companies. Because such loans incurred an across-the-board 8 percent minimum capital requirement, or 100 percent risk weight, whether the counterparty was General Electric or a local electrician, it was profitable to shift those loans with an economic capital requirement of less than 8 percent off balance sheet.

Conversely, if the real risk on a loan was higher than the regulatory capital requirement, it was more profitable to simply retain the asset on the balance sheet, provided it was priced correctly.

The scope for regulatory arbitrage was magnified precisely at this time by rapid technological advances in computing and telecommunications as well as theoretical advances in option pricing models.[4] It became possible to slice, dice, repackage, and redistribute every conceivable type of risk. These financial innovations prompted the Basel Committee to issue the 1996 Market Risk Amendment and subsequently the New Capital Framework (Basel II) in 2005.

The ad hoc nature of the standardized risk weight approach under Basel I set banks clamoring for a more advanced regulatory framework, incorporating greater convergence between regulatory and economic capital. This imperative is addressed in the Basel II framework: "International Convergence of Capital Measurement and Capital Standards."

State of the art prudential regulation necessitates striking a delicate balance along the continua of effective prudential supervision versus banks' economic risk-taking function on one hand and regulatory capital versus economic capital on the other. Ideally this would achieve convergence of regulatory and economic capital across the efficiency dimension while providing a framework across the effectiveness dimension within which depositors, taxpayers, and the financial system's systemic health is protected, without impinging on banks' economically essential risk-taking activities.

Integrating such diverse criteria was made feasible by moving away from the oversimplification of standardized risk weights applied only to the banking book, as under the original Basel I Accord, toward a more granular risk-based approach, supported by three pillars. The three-pillar structure of minimum capital requirements, supervisory review, and market discipline applies uniformly across banking organizations and jurisdictions, as it forms the foundation of the risk-based approach, but banks can choose whether to implement a standardized approach or a more sophisticated internal models approach.

For large, sophisticated banks, the value proposition implicit in aligning regulatory and economic capital via the internal models approach was irrefutable. This framework lays the foundation for granular risk measurement, progressive risk management policies, and risk appetite refinement. Banks were further incentivized by the prospect of being rewarded for their implementation efforts by the expectation of lower regulatory capital requirements.

Pillar 1 of the Basel II Accord improves on the original accord by linking the sensitivity of risk-based minimum capital requirements to empirical measures of credit and operational risk. These risk parameters, such as the probability of default (PD) attached to any particular loan and its consequent loss given default (LGD), are estimated by the bank itself, subject to supervisory guidance and review. The proviso is that estimated risk parameters should also pass the *use test*—that is, actually be applied by the bank to its internal risk management processes. By more accurately reflecting the risk reduction effects of securitization, credit derivatives, and guarantees, Pillar 1 incentivizes banks to hedge their credit risks. Additionally, there is now also explicit recognition of the importance of operational risk.

Pillar 2 focuses on the principles of supervisory review, creating a platform for dialogue to align the quality of capital adequacy assessment by both bank and supervisor. Pillar 2 covers all risks not addressed within Pillar 1, such as interest rate risk in the banking book, liquidity risk, and concentration risk. While the goal of Pillar 2 is to ensure adequate capital against the full set of risks to which a bank is exposed, it explicitly acknowledges that increased capital can never be a substitute for best practice risk control and management.

Pillar 3 increases the transparency of banks to the financial markets by public disclosure of risk-based capital ratios, portfolio credit quality, and risk management practices.

To those in the banking industry, Basel II has represented nothing less than a revolution in risk measurement and risk management. The three-pillar approach has enabled banks to understand and quantify their credit, market, and operational risks. Economic capital can then be allocated to each risk position by estimating loss distributions at a specified confidence interval. For example, an A-rated bank would typically target an aggregated value at risk across its risk positions of about 30 basis points over a one-year horizon, or equivalently a risk of ruin in one year of every 333 years of operations. Qualitative requirements under Pillar 2 allow this bank to demonstrate the reliability of its capital adequacy calculations to its national supervisor. Communication of banks' granular credit and operational risk positions under Pillar 3 to depositors, shareholders, analysts, and rating agencies ensures that the bank retains its rating and continues to enjoy a healthy deposit stream and competitive funding.

APPLICATION TO SOLVENCY II: REGULATION

For the foreseeable future, the Solvency II initiative is likely to remain the most significant challenge and opportunity confronting the insurance industry. Within the European Union (EU), the framework will establish prudential standards likely to remain in force for a considerable period. There are, however, no grounds for complacency on the part of insurers in other jurisdictions. A great many regulatory initiatives drafted in the EU historically have been adopted either substantially or in full in other jurisdictions. Quite aside from the regulatory drivers, the implementation of Basel II has demonstrated the compelling commercial logic of precommitment to the new framework. Based on banks' experience with Basel II, the latter part of this chapter highlights salient instances of the value that insurers can expect to derive from early adoption, as distinct from the mere necessity of regulatory compliance.

From a regulatory point of view, substantial learning from Basel II has already occurred, which is reflected in the composition and requirements of the Solvency II Directive. At a conceptual level, the formulation of the directive would seem to have benefited from and even improved upon (from an insurance perspective) Basel II in three important ways.

First, the most obvious similarity between the two regimes is the application of the three-pillar framework to Solvency II, with the choice of adopting a standardized approach or the more rigorous internal models approach. While Pillars 2 and 3 are broadly comparable in scope and purpose to Basel II, Pillar 1 differs substantially. Because the risk landscape confronting an insurance entity is so much broader and encompasses greater uncertainty, the directive aims to include *all* quantifiable risks under Pillar 1. In addition to the risks covered in Basel II, insurance entities need to quantify risks associated with asset liability management, underwriting, catastrophe, and biometric risks. A broader range of risks are thus specified, across all assets and liabilities while the notion of principles-based regulation is retained. There are no prescriptions as to the design of internal models. Insurers have the discretion to construct models in a manner consistent with the way risk is managed within the firm, reflecting underlying economic and market reality.

The second improvement over Basel II stems from Solvency II's requirement to hold regulatory capital against risks emanating from both the asset and the liability side of the balance sheet in an integrated way, whereas Basel II focuses only on assets.

The third improvement is the specification of regulatory capital as a range of regulatory intervention rather than a point target. While the SCR remains the target capital requirement under normal market conditions, Solvency II additionally stipulates a minimum capital requirement, below which the regulator could place the firm under administration. This approach may somewhat alleviate the procyclicality inherent in insurance (and banking) supervision. This solvency "continuum" enables the regulator to force the insurer to act prior to hitting a minimum capital requirement, which allows for the smoothing out of any impending crisis, over a longer period of time, with the advantage of early warning indicators.

APPLICATION TO SOLVENCY II: BUSINESS LOGIC

For most retail, corporate, and investment banks, the Basel II implementation experience has been an extreme test of their suppleness in response to a program spanning vastly divergent dimensions of the organization. This challenge has been compounded because the Basel II change program is the most comprehensive of its kind to date. Several aspects of the Basel II protocol provide unique insight into the problems faced by banks and the issues pertaining to Solvency II.

The first key dimension of the Basel II regime is that it is in fact a regime. It is a regulatory requirement that implies specific stipulations. First, it had to be implemented by a predetermined date at a business, technology, and data level. The second broad stipulation is that a regulatory regime has specific dates or milestones associated with it. The project implementation *must* keep pace with the stipulated progress dates. There have been very few instances in industry where a change program timeline has been externally imposed to the extent we have seen in Basel II. The third broad stipulation is that it is competitive because all banks are obliged to implement the regime. Both Basel II and Solvency II are designed in such a way that those institutions gaining the greatest insight to their risks by giving the implementation their full commitment are likely to enjoy the greatest capital relief or benefit by shedding unprofitable risks.

In clarification of the latter point, it is often stated that because the standardized approach to the calculation of SCR is intended to yield a conservative estimate of required capital, the value proposition of implementing the internal models approach is clear, as this will release capital. This may or may not be the case. Certain banks implementing Basel II did in fact realize substantial capital savings. But the irrefutable logic driving the substantial investment required for the internal models approach is rather the increased risk sensitivity of the regulatory capital calculation. Internal models provide management with a tool to gauge their desired capital cushion and risk appetite and also a benchmark for price-volume optimization and risk-based pricing.

The second dimension to the regime is that it applies at a group-wide level. The first few pages of the Basel II Accord are not about the regulations per se but rather the interpretation of the regulations in relation to cross-border banking and multinational banking groups. This primary emphasis on consolidation is central to the Accord's principal objective of promoting the soundness and stability of the international banking system by creating a level playing field for all participants. The group-wide application of Solvency II on a consolidated basis is of crucial importance. The European Council has for the time being deleted the group support provisions while retaining the group solvency provisions. SCR is therefore also required at the level of host country subsidiaries rather than only on a consolidated basis at the level of the home-country parent, undermining the full diversification potential of the directive. It is the express wish of a majority of players in the industry that the group support provisions are reintroduced in 2015 when the question is reviewed.

Nevertheless, Solvency II deals with all types of insurance companies, all types of insurance assets, and all types of insurance liabilities. There is a clear parallel here to Basel II since retail, corporate, and investment banking are almost completely different businesses, yet are governed under a single directive. They operate differently, and they have different personalities, different degrees of focus on data and technology, and widely divergent management styles.

A retail bank tends to be a high-volume business employing a technology-centric focus. Management objectives tend to emphasize technology, efficiency ratios, and analytics as the foundation of optimal portfolio-wide decision making.

A corporate bank, however, is a relationship-driven bank. It is staffed predominantly by highly paid professionals who build relationships with corporations, offering both advisory and debt structuring services in competition with its peers.

An investment bank also employs a technology-centric focus but in the sense of intellectual property technologies, which are structuring concepts and ways to structure deals. Like corporate banking, investment banking is highly relationship driven, employing exceptionally talented individuals to create value-added services for clients.

Corporate banking and investment banking both tend to be low-volume, high-value businesses. Technologically they are often driven by spreadsheets; the data storage systems and the corporate memory per se are often of much lower sophistication than is typically found within a retail bank. Much of the data and technology found in a corporate or investment bank are personal-productivity driven. These institutions typically buy a piece of software for a particular banker or group of bankers to solve a particular problem. In this environment, it does not matter if different departments use different systems because they are focused on solving particular low-volume, high-value problems.

Basel II is a unique project in banking history, crossing the divide between retail, corporate, and investment banking. Important implications for Solvency II stem from the fact that Basel II is group wide and that it insists on a single architecture and a single set of reports, where all of these assets are reported in a single regulatory return. A similar challenge awaits insurers as they prepare to implement

Solvency II across life, non-life, and health, for all assets and liabilities, on a consolidated basis.

The third and arguably most important key dimension of Basel II is that it intersects the three critical components within a bank: business units, information technology (IT), and risk management. The Basel II regulations and Solvency II Directive necessarily intersect with all three of these disciplines, since the successful implementation of both requires embedding the regulations and directives into business practice and process, information technology systems, data processes, and within the risk management function as a whole. The reason for this is the use test common to both regimes.

The Basel II use test insists that calculated risk parameters, such as probability of default (PD), loss given default (LGD), exposure at default (EAD), and effective maturity (M) may not be calculated in a vacuum. Paragraph 444 of the Basel Accord explicitly states that it is unacceptable to calculate risk parameters exclusively for the purpose of qualifying for the internal models approach but that "ratings and default and loss estimates must play an essential role in the credit approval, risk management, internal capital allocations, and corporate governance functions of banks." In effect, such parameters must be calculated using banks' actual data, actual experience of defaults and losses and recoveries, and using actual bank decision-making processes.

When one builds a PD model, for example, one is required to use the underlying data that the business unit already use to make business decisions. Moreover, the PD model results must be used by the business unit in future decision making in a manner consistent with the parameterization itself. One must be able to demonstrate to the regulator via the concept of the use test that real intelligence has been garnered from one's own data and own models and that such intelligence is being applied to business decision making. These decisions include:

- Accept/decline
- Pricing
- Performance metrics
- Performance attribution to bankers

- Calculation of regulatory capital
- Calculation of economic capital

For the PD model, a threshold must be established as a bank credit policy, above which any new deal application is rejected (i.e., it is a poor deal because it has a high probability of default). One must be able to demonstrate to the regulator that the implemented threshold is determined against the PD scale and the distribution of PDs estimated for those customers. One must further be able to demonstrate that the pricing of a loan—that is, the number of basis points above the swaps yield curve—is logically associated with the PD of that obligor itself.

The implication of the use test is that Basel II and Solvency II are not merely compliance issues but rather clearly articulate a business case both deserving of and necessitating early executive buy-in to the change program. Executive articulation of the regulatory and commercial drivers at the outset should preclude any tendency toward the attrition of budget and resources to shorter-term "priorities." By ensuring that sound project management is in place to allocate resources and responsibilities for specific aspects of delivery, coupled with clear project governance to ensure cohesion across business units and functional areas, management creates an environment conducive to leveraging a substantial regulatory investment into a fully functional enterprise-wide risk management tool.

Executive sponsorship of an integrated holistic approach to the implementation of Solvency II is crucial to its ultimate success and potential for competitive advantage. The most important insight for insurers from the implementation of Basel II is that many banks failed to achieve Advanced Internal Ratings–Based (AIRB) compliance because they lacked such an integrated holistic approach. These banks tended to view Basel II as a compliance/risk management program, an IT issue, or a business unit problem. None of these three approaches works individually.

To achieve success, business units needed to link all their business processes and their decision making to the regulatory stipulations and, where necessary, build business processes around meeting the minimum requirements. The second group that had to be involved was the Basel II Programme Office, which typically originated from what used to be the risk management department. Risk management professionals had to interpret the requirements in order to accept existing models or modify them, build new models, and ensure that asset classification problems were properly addressed. The IT department's input was required because an organized automated process was needed for data flows, logic, and data architecture.

"Accurate, complete, and consistent data" is a prerequisite to building internal models that can accurately capture economic reality. In the run-up to Basel II implementation, many banks made the mistake of focusing all their energies on perfecting the Pillar 1 capital calculations, significantly underestimating the extent of data quality issues and the effort required to fix them. As the implementation deadline loomed, many were forced to resort to short-term tactical patches. Consequently, they now have to cope with ongoing unresolved data issues. This has caused wholly unnecessary additional operating costs and higher capital requirements than otherwise would be the case.

A frequent and critical misconception prevailing at the inception of Basel II conflated the framework to an IT issue. Many banks assumed incorrectly that it was simply a matter of selecting a software vendor and purchasing an off-the-shelf application. But going live with a new regulatory reporting framework requires the integration of historic data, consistent current data, and internal models for all business units.

The successful implementation of Solvency II will likewise mean that a dedicated team of actuarial modelers, project managers, risk managers, IT professionals, and data specialists will be needed. Insurers that delay embarking on the journey may find at critical junctures that the availability of such specialists has dried up, causing further delays.

For successful implementation, it is critical that early executive buy-in is obtained, preferably with the change management program championed by a chief risk officer, to integrate all three aspects in a firm-wide project. To avoid obsessive focus on particular functional components, the project should enjoy executive budgeting, executive reporting, and the full commitment through role clarity across group business clusters, IT, and risk management. Insurers that have the foresight to recognize the potential pitfalls experienced by banks have an opportunity to leverage their considerable regulatory investment. By achieving early compliance with the internal models approach, they will be able to avoid relegation to the higher regulatory capital requirements of the standardized approach. Furthermore, they will be able to optimize their risk return profile and create sustained competitive advantage by early identification of the most profitable opportunities.

LESSONS FROM THE CREDIT CRISIS

The credit crisis demonstrated to the banking industry the value and necessity of integrated enterprise-wide risk management. In this context, implementation of the new Solvency II regime has far greater implications and consequences for insurance undertakings than mere regulatory compliance. It is above all a journey to sustained competitive advantage. Those institutions gaining the greatest insight into their risks by giving the implementation their full commitment are likely to enjoy the greatest capital relief or benefit by shedding unprofitable risks. This observation is borne out by the Senior Supervisors' Group report, "Observations on Risk Management Practices during the Recent Market Turbulence,"[5] on the effectiveness of risk management at major global financial services entities during the crisis.[6]

The report was undertaken in response to a request from the Financial Stability Forum, whose mission is to promote international financial stability, improve the functioning of markets, and reduce systemic risk through information exchange and international cooperation in financial supervision and surveillance. The report's primary purpose was to evaluate the effectiveness of current risk management practices as applied at financial institutions, both during and before the credit crisis, to inform potential future changes in supervisory requirements.

Analysis was conducted on 11 of the largest banking and securities institutions to search for differentiation between risk management practices associated with positive or negative performance. The observations of the report reflect supervisory judgment based on a questionnaire, systematic discussions, and information otherwise available to supervisors to ascertain:

- How proactive senior management was in response to a shifting risk landscape
- Market and credit risk management practices, in particular understanding the risks in traded and counterparty exposures, valuing complex and illiquid instruments, and hedging exposures
- The extent and effectiveness of liquidity risk management practices in identifying and responding to increased vulnerability in a stressed environment

Four firm-wide risk management practices were found to differentiate performance:

1. "Effective firm-wide risk identification and analysis"
2. "Consistent application of independent and rigorous valuation practices across the firm"
3. "Effective management of funding liquidity, capital, and the balance sheet"
4. "Informative and responsive risk measurement and management reporting and practices"

Firms that were found to cope more easily with the challenges presented by the market turmoil shared quantitative and qualitative information effectively across the organization. Maintaining dialogue between C-level management, business owners, and control functions permitted these organizations to recognize the potential sources of risk as early as 2006. Early identification shielded these firms from the worst losses, since they had time to monitor evolving market conditions and implement an appropriate firm-wide containment strategy, either by reducing exposures or by hedging risks.

Firms whose share price and capital adequacy came under severe pressure generally lacked stringent internal processes to challenge existing valuations: Senior tranches of collateralized debt obligations (CDOs) continued to be priced at par despite evidence of underlying collateral deterioration and liquidity strains; they relied exclusively on the views of the ratings agencies; and they underestimated the potential for increased asset correlations under market strain. By contrast, better performers had developed in-house techniques to assess the quality of assets underlying securities, because they were skeptical of ratings assigned to complex structured credit products by the agencies. By applying these values consistently across the firm to own and counterparty positions, they were able to get a much clearer picture of their exposures.

Some institutions had moved toward enterprise-wide management of their consolidated balance sheet, funding liquidity, and capital position by closer alignment of the treasury and risk management functions. This enabled a global view of the changing firm-wide contingent liquidity risk. Internal pricing mechanisms were used to incentivize business units to exercise control over balance sheet growth and liquidity by charging business units for contingent liquidity risk. The perceived contingent liquidity risk disciplined firms to adhere to limits through evolving market conditions and in some cases even entirely avoid some business lines, such as CDO warehousing, by outweighing potential returns.

Better performers relied on a wider range of risk measurement tools, incorporating a much broader range of assumptions. Adaptive risk management processes and systems allowed managers at these firms to quickly change assumptions to reflect current conditions. These firms also relied on a wider range of risk measures—for example, by comparing gross versus net positions under various scenarios or by integrating market and counterparty risk positions across business units.

At a macro level, the International Monetary Fund's October 2008 World Economic Outlook cautioned that recent historical evidence seems to suggest that economies characterized by a greater degree of arm's-length financing tend to experience financial crises of far greater amplitude than more relationship-based systems. The reason is simple. Funding increasingly opaque and complex assets, such as CDOs, for example, by relying on short-term liabilities, such as overnight wholesale funding, which is prone to sudden reversals in times of stress, amplifies procyclicality.

The trend toward securitization in arm's-length financial systems created the illusion of spreading risk by offsetting the idiosyncratic risks inherent to more relationship-based systems with portfolio diversification effects. In theory this may be possible, but financial institutions neglected to independently verify the risk of their exposures. A lack of information and understanding of the value and risks of exposures played a significant role in amplifying the credit crisis.

Insurers may counter that procyclicality concerns are of little relevance to them. Given the longer-term nature of their liabilities, capital adequacy can be reviewed at a more leisurely pace. But this claim ignores a key lesson from the credit crisis: Balance sheet optimization is incomplete in the absence of a comprehensive understanding of the potential volatility and losses of underlying exposures. While insurance solvency as a concept remains opaque to investors, insurers likewise are vulnerable to sudden reversals of fortune.

In conclusion, effective risk management encompasses the understanding, timely identification, and management of risk. The actual measurement of risk is of little use in the absence of these activities. Additionally, the probability of managing risk successfully seems to be greater where relationships play some role at transaction origination, reducing opacity by creating an element of reciprocal trust.

CONCLUSION

This chapter has attempted to present an unbiased account of the continuing relevance of financial regulation despite the cynicism and suspicion engendered by the financial crisis. While the structure of Solvency II is loosely based on Basel II's three-pillar structure of quantitative requirements, supervisory review, and market disclosure, Solvency II represents a change in thinking and in logic away from some of the pitfalls of Basel II. Solvency II's principles-based construct has been carefully thought out, developed over many years by collaboration among the European Commission, member states, and the insurance industry, and holds the promise of creating a more stable insurance industry through a common set of standards and principles. Embracing the opportunity of such an integrated enterprise-wide risk management project presents a rare opportunity for individual insurers to entrench sustained competitive advantages.

CHAPTER 5

The Solvency II
Directive in Brief

WHAT IS SOLVENCY II?

Even prior to the financial crisis that began in 2008, Solvency II had matured to the extent that industry observers recognized its significance in mitigating against future financial calamity. The financial crisis reiterated the necessity for financial services organizations to reassess their risk management practices. This chapter covers the Solvency II Directive Framework, including the various requirements associated with the three-pillar structure.

Solvency II is a fundamental review of the capital adequacy regime for the European insurance industry. The purpose of this legislation is to ensure the financial stability of insurance companies, taking into consideration their assets and liabilities, and to replace the current Solvency I requirements. As has been covered in previous chapters, Solvency II has borrowed heavily from the regulatory framework first installed in Basel II. Although the directives have similar frameworks and measurements, Solvency II has the potential for far more complexities, not least of which is a significant internal model validation challenge. While Basel II has been adopted by countries throughout the world, including those outside the European Union (EU), at present Solvency II will only be implemented within the EU, although regulators around the world are watching developments with interest.

The primary principle of the EU is to create an effective single market across all 27 EU countries. Solvency II is one of the key components of the European Commission's Action Plan for the Financial Services. It will consolidate the 14 existing European insurance directives and introduces an entirely new harmonized European solvency regime.

Speaking at the launch of the Solvency II draft directive framework in July 2007, Charlie McCreevy of the European Commission for Internal Market and Services said, "We are setting a world-leading standard that requires insurers to focus on managing all the risks they face and enables them to operate much more efficiently. It's good news for consumers, for the insurance industry, and the EU economy as a whole."[1] The directive was officially approved by the European Parliament on April 22, 2009, and the proposed implementation date is January 1, 2013.

Solvency II's primary objective is the protection of policyholders and beneficiaries. It strengthens policyholder protection through capital requirements, which also provide early warning of deterioration in solvency levels. Other directive objectives are to:

- Deepen integration of the European insurance market.
- Improve the international competitiveness of EU insurers.
- Promote better regulation through a principles-based and risk-sensitive solvency regime.
- Align capital requirements to a company's risk profile.
- Instill risk awareness into governance, operations, and decision making.

The Solvency II Directive will apply to all insurance and reinsurance companies with annual premiums greater than €5 million that conduct business in the European Economic Area, which covers all 27 EU countries, plus Norway, Liechtenstein, and Iceland. Companies with premium revenue under €5 million may choose to opt in to the

Solvency II Directive. The Solvency II regulations will also be applicable to non-EU subsidiaries of EU-based insurers. The directive will not differentiate between types of insurance companies and will apply to all stock (listed or unlisted), mutual, and cooperative insurers. There are a few exceptions to the legislation; most apply to insurance and reinsurance companies that were in run-off before December 2007.[2]

SOLVENCY II IS PRINCIPLES-BASED

Although the directive has "Solvency" in its title, it explicitly states that capital is not the only (or necessarily the best) way to mitigate failure. This theory is supported by the Committee of European Insurance and Occupational Pensions Supervisors (CEIOPS) and leading analysts. Studies by CEIOPS have found that the primary cause of insurance company failure is poor management decisions and inappropriate risk decisions, not inadequate capital. Industry concurs. Simon Harris, Moody's managing director for European insurance, is quoted as saying, "The purpose of Solvency II is not necessarily to strengthen the industry's capital base, but more to ensure that sufficient regulatory and internal risk management controls are in place to enable management and regulators to more fully understand and control the dynamics of the industry's risk profile."[3]

Under Solvency II, firms will be required to meet regulatory principles rather than rules. The proposed regime acknowledges that some types of risk are best addressed through good governance rather than by simply allocating additional solvency capital. One such principle allows firms to use internal models to calculate the solvency capital requirements (SCR), subject to regulatory approval. Criteria should not be so onerous as to dissuade firms from applying for model recognition. In particular, if models are to pass the use test of being integrated into firms' risk management, validation criteria must be reasonably flexible. This flexibility will help ensure that criteria do not quickly become obsolete or unduly restrict modeling innovation. One way of achieving flexibility is to set high-level principles, in particular relating to model governance, and a requirement that the model output must be of such a level of regulatory capital that satisfies the SCR. Flexibility would have the advantage of allowing supervisors to recognize models that firms have already developed, where appropriate.

The implementation of Solvency II will have important consequences for the way in which insurance companies and supervisory authorities operate in the future. Requiring all firms to conduct an individual risk and capital assessment will act as a powerful tool to encourage and reward more comprehensive risk management practices. This, in turn, will lead to a much better assessment and alignment of actual capital needed by an insurance company to meet its risks. The new solvency rules thus will inevitably shift business attitude from a compliance-based culture to a risk management culture. Supervisory authorities for their part will have to become more knowledgeable and develop the necessary skills to assess risk governance and internal models. As a consequence, these bodies may need to attract people with different skills and acquire new resources. Cooperation in the development of further implementation measures, and in the validation of group internal models, as well as peer reviews, will contribute to improving supervisory convergence, which should ultimately also be in the interest of the insurance industry and of policyholders.

PARTIAL AND INTERNAL MODELS

One of the key components of the Solvency II Directive is that it allows insurance companies to use their own internal models rather than the standard model approach. The internal models approach allows a more customized assessment of a particular business and its potential risk than can ever be replicated in a standard model. For most insurers, the hoped-for advantage of using an internal model is that it could lead to lower capital requirements than the standard formula, but increased risk sensitivity is also a powerful incentive. There may also be potential benefits associated with financial strength, according to the rating agencies.

The International Association of Insurance Supervisors defines an internal model as "a risk management system developed by an insurer to analyze the overall position, to quantify risks and to determine the economic capital needed to meet these risks."[4] A key component of an internal model is the approach used to quantify and measure risk exposure.

Solvency II also includes the concept of partial internal models, which are part internal models and part standard model approach. For many companies, especially smaller ones, a partial model may be more appropriate and cost effective than a full internal model. Some firms may be required to develop a (full or partial) internal model if the supervisor considers that their risk profile deviates significantly from that assumed for the standard formula SCR. It is also likely that some firms may come under peer pressure to develop internal models to keep up with similar firms that have a more sophisticated approach.

Insurance companies employing an internal or partial model approach must obtain approval from the regulators. The Solvency II Directive stipulates that the supervisor will decide on the application within six months of receipt. Perhaps the most important criteria for internal model approval, as alluded to earlier, is the ability of the insurer to demonstrate that it passes the use test. The use test requires that the model is embedded within the system of governance and is a key tool in the insurer's decision-making processes. Also, the internal models must meet particular statistical quality standards and be capable of being calibrated to the one-year 99.5 percent level specified in the standard model approach for the SCR calculation.

Supervisors will require firms to run their internal models on relevant benchmark portfolios and use assumptions based on external rather than internal data in order to verify the calibration and to check that it is in line with accepted market practice. Even when approval is given, insurers must provide the supervisor with an estimate of the standard formula SCR for two additional years. Finally, for internal model approval, insurers must have processes in place to ensure that the model continues to reflect their risk profile and that the models and processes are regularly validated and documented.

ECONOMIC CAPITAL

Capital adequacy may be considered from three points of view: those of the insurance entity and its shareholders, the rating agencies, and the regulator. From the point of view of the insurance entity and the ratings agencies, adequate capital, or economic capital, is considered to be the risk capital required to preclude default or absorb losses over one year to the desired confidence level, for example, 99.97 percent for an AA-rated entity. Solvency II requires regulatory capital to be held against a 1-in-200-years risk of ruin probability, or 99.5 percent.

Regulatory capital refers to the capital required by the directive to protect the rights and benefits of the individual policyholder. Economic capital is an acknowledgment by the firm as a legal entity of the need to maximize its returns, taking into account the need to put capital aside against unexpected losses. The two may differ, and indeed regularly do differ, as has been illustrated under the Basel II framework. However, as it is a more principles-based than rules-based framework, Solvency II better aligns the economic interests of a nameless and faceless community of shareholders with those of individual policyholders.

Both regulatory and economic capital under Solvency II recognize that an insurer faces risks on both the asset and the liability side of its balance sheet. The raison d'être of the regulatory capital point of view may be considered to be the protection of policyholders. If available regulatory capital should fall below the minimum capital requirement (MCR), the supervisor may force the insurer to close to new business, run-off assets and liabilities, or transfer liabilities to another insurer. The MCR thus ensures that sufficient financial resources are available to compensate another insurer for assuming the liabilities. The economic capital point of view, being an internal capital adequacy point of view, is concerned with the continuity of the insurance entity as a going concern and also should be constrained by assumptions as to evolving risk appetite and near-term management actions.

THE ECONOMIC BALANCE SHEET

The assessment of solvency in the directive is based on a total, market-consistent economic balance sheet. That is, the capital requirements must consider risk originating from both sides of the balance sheet. It is widely recognized that the most appropriate basis for evaluating assets is on a market-value basis. Therefore, to ensure consistency, liabilities are also valued at a market-consistent value. Moreover, the economic balance sheet clearly distinguishes between the underlying asset and liability values and the capital required for solvency purposes.

Market-consistent value of assets (MVA) is defined as the amount at which assets should be valued if they could be transferred to a knowledgeable willing party in an arm's-length transaction. Market-consistent value of liabilities (MVL) is derived from the cost of managing the risks underlying the business on an ongoing basis. In most cases, insurance liabilities are not actively traded. Therefore, the MVA cannot be determined directly from capital markets and must be calculated using market-consistent techniques.

One such technique is the replicating portfolio, which is the portfolio of assets that most closely matches the corresponding liability cash flows. In the absence of arbitrage, and if the liability cash flows could be matched exactly, the MVL will exactly equal the market value of the replicating portfolio. The replicating portfolio must be set up to mimic all future cash flows excluding profits. Future cash outflows are assessed net of expected future premium inflows to allow for the expected run-off of policies due to claims, lapses, and surrenders.

The three main components of the market-consistent economic balance sheet for the Solvency II Directive therefore are the MVA, the MVL, and the SCR. Excess capital available to the insurer will be the difference between the MVA and the sum of the MVL and the SCR.

STRUCTURE OF THE DIRECTIVE

Inspired by banking's Basel II legislation, Solvency II uses a similar three-pillar structure covering both quantitative elements and qualitative aspects that influence an insurer's risk standing. Pillar 1 consists of the quantitative requirements; Pillar 2, the supervisory activities; and Pillar 3, the reporting and public disclosure requirements. The three pillars should not, however, be looked at in isolation, because there is a clear interaction among them.

The most important objective of Solvency II is that it should provide supervisors with the appropriate tools and powers to assess the overall solvency of all insurance and reinsurance companies based on a prospective and risk-oriented approach. It will therefore consist not only of the Pillar 1 quantitative elements but will also cover qualitative aspects that influence the insurer's risk standing, such as managerial capacity, internal risk control, and risk monitoring processes. Transparency in the quantification of risk and of risk governance practiced by insurers is enhanced through Pillar 3 disclosure requirements, which also include the requirement to make certain information available to public scrutiny. The next sections cover the three pillars in more detail.

Pillar 1

Pillar 1 defines the quantitative requirements of the Solvency II Directive and contains two key features: the solvency capital requirement and the minimum capital requirement. These calculations are made once a quarter for the following one-year period and are reported to insurers' respective supervisors.[5] As part of the calculations, the Solvency II Directive states that assets and liabilities should be measured on a consistent basis for solvency purposes and that this basis should be the market value. To determine the MVL, a market value margin (MVM) needs to be added to the expected present value of future liability cash flows.

The SCR is the risk-based capital requirement that guarantees the minimum capital required to maintain appropriate policyholder protection and is a key solvency control level. The SCR reflects a level of capital that enables an insurer to absorb significant unforeseen losses. It will be set at a level that leaves less than a 1-in-200 chance (99.5 percent) that capital will prove inadequate over the next 12 months. When an insurer does not meet the SCR, it will be required to increase the amount of capital necessary to cover the SCR, based on a definitive and realizable plan approved by its supervisor.

The SCR calculation takes into account all quantifiable risk that an insurer may encounter, including underwriting risk, market risk, credit risk, and operational risk. In addition, to encourage effective risk management, the SCR must take into account reinsurance and other forms of risk mitigation.

Solvency II will allow insurers to calculate the SCR using either the standard model or internal model approach discussed earlier. The standard model approach will apply a relatively simple formula that will relate capital requirements to key risk categories. Insurers using an internal model approach will require regulatory approval.

The adjusted SCR is the SCR plus any capital add-ons to account for risks that were not fully assessed in the SCR. These add-ons can be imposed by the supervisor and result in a higher capital requirement for deficiencies in the risk profile of an insurer's business for the purposes of calculating the SCR. Capital add-ons are covered later in this chapter.

As alluded to earlier, the MCR indicates a level of capital below which ultimate supervisory action is initiated if an attempted recovery has been deemed unsuccessful. This action may result either in closing the insurer to new business and run-off of the existing book of business or transferring the portfolio to another insurance company. The MCR is calculated quarterly, and the confidence levels are set at between 80 and 90 percent of the SCR.

The supervisory measures defined in the Solvency II Directive are based on a ladder of intervention. These measures denote the actions that a supervisor will take if certain capital thresholds are breached. Table 5.1 summarizes the ladder of intervention and the necessary options available to the supervisors.

Table 5.1 Solvency II Ladder of Intervention

	Additional Reporting	Financial Recovery Plan	Closure to New Business	Authorization Withdrawn
No breach (adequate capital)	Not required	Not required	Not required	Not required
Breach of adjusted SCR	Required	Possible	Not required	Not required
Breach of SCR	Required	Required	Possible	Not required
Breach of MCR	Required	Required	Required	Possible

Source: FSA, "Solvency II: A New Framework for Prudential Regulation of Insurance in the EU," www.fsa.gov.uk/pubs/international/solvency2_discussion.pdf.

Pillar 2

One of the problems with the existing Solvency I regulations was the failure to provide supervisors and regulators with enough warning or sufficient powers to intervene in the event of a potentially insolvent insurer. Pillar 2 addresses this issue by assessing the effectiveness of each insurer's risk management procedures. The key requirement is that there must be an effective governance (including risk management) system, owned and implemented by senior management. There are two main requirements for Pillar 2: the Own Risk and Solvency Assessment (ORSA) and the Supervisory Review Process (SRP).

The Solvency II Directive requires that each insurer, as part of its risk management processes, must have a regular procedure for assessing its overall solvency needs. This assessment, which should be performed at least annually, is known as the ORSA process and has two main goals. The first is to embed into the insurer's risk management processes an internal assessment procedure to ensure that it satisfies the Solvency II requirements. Producing the ORSA is not just a box-ticking exercise; insurers must demonstrate that the assessment has an influence on strategic business decision making. The second objective of the ORSA process is to create a supervisory tool for the regulatory authorities, who must be informed of the results of the insurer's own risk and solvency assessment. According to CEIOPS, the ORSA process aims at enhancing awareness of the interrelationships between the risks an undertaking is currently exposed to, or may face in the long term, and the internal capital needs that follow from this risk exposure.

The ORSA process should complement the insights gained from the Pillar 1 quantitative calculations. Insurers should highlight areas where they believe the assessment deviates significantly from the SCR calculations, especially where an internal model has been deployed.

The ORSA process should also include a forward-looking perspective or what-if process to help insurers better understand their risk exposures and how these might evolve and interact over the medium term, beyond the Pillar 1 quantitative calculations. By using stress and scenario testing, and through a combination of capital and risk projections, insurers can create contingency and mitigation plans that set out the options for managing and maintaining their capital and solvency positions in line with their desired risk appetite.

The ORSA process should be a key tool to foster a risk management culture within a company and should be linked to other forecasting activities, such as business planning, product design, and longer-term capital management. Ultimate responsibility rests with an insurer's executive board, since all the components of the ORSA must be captured in a report signed off by the administrative body and presented to the supervisors for review.[6]

From a supervisory perspective, the ORSA process will play an important role in ensuring that the executive board maintains appropriate understanding and oversight of its risk exposures. ORSA will also influence a supervisor's decision as to whether an insurer should have a capital add-on applied. As a result, the ORSA process is set to be a key driver for embedding enterprise risk management into the business. The reports that are produced are likely to be among the most important aspects of supervisory review under Solvency II.

As previously emphasized, Solvency II insurers will be required to meet regulatory principles rather than rules. Hence Solvency II acknowledges that some types of risk are best addressed through good governance rather than by allocating additional solvency capital. Thus the purpose of the SRP is to ensure that the supervisor regularly evaluates the insurer against both the qualitative and the quantitative Solvency II requirements and guarantees the insurer's compliance with the directive.

The SRP considers six main areas:

1. System of governance and risk assessment

2. Technical provisions

3. Capital requirements

4. Investment rules

5. Quality and quantity of own funds

6. Use of a full or partial internal model, if deployed

Through the SRP, the supervisor will assess the ability of an insurer's system of governance to identify, assess, and manage the risks and potential risks it faces as a business. The supervisor will have the power to force firms to remedy any weaknesses and deficiencies it identifies in their system of governance, including strategies, processes, and reporting procedures, in order to give greater confidence in the overall solvency position. In exceptional cases, the supervisor will also be able to impose a capital add-on. Supervisors will be required to remove capital add-ons promptly when associated deficiencies have been rectified.

The supervisor will determine the frequency and exact scope of each review and will use monitoring tools to identify any financial deterioration of a firm. The objective is to assess a firm's ability to withstand possible adverse events, catastrophes, or future changes in economic conditions.

As defined by CEIOPS:

> The capital add-on is a supervisory tool that allows supervisors to require insurers to hold capital in addition to the Solvency Capital Requirement as originally calculated by the standard formula or an internal model, provided the supervisory review process leads to a conclusion that the level of required solvency capital held by the company is insufficient or that the company needs to remedy qualitative deficiencies.[7]

The capital add-on will be neither routinely nor commonly applied but evaluated on a case-by-case basis by the insurer's supervisor. Although a capital add-on is anticipated to be a temporary measure, it could remain in place for many years if the risk profile of the undertaking deviates from the assumptions underlying the SCR because the partial or full internal model is deficient or because of risk governance deficiencies. The contrary is, of course, also true: The supervisor may require the firm to develop a full or partial internal model if the standard formula does not accurately capture the insurer's risk profile.

Pillar 3

Pillar 3 of the Solvency II Directive covers disclosure, both privately to supervisors and publicly to other stakeholders. In defining the Pillar 3 requirements, special attention was given to some of the changes being proposed on a global basis, such as the common standards for solvency rules and principles as set forth by the International Association of Insurance Supervisors, new financial reporting standards for insurance companies from the International Accounting Standards Board, and a classification of risks and best estimate calculation methodology for technical provisions by the International Association of Actuaries.

The new disclosure documents required as part of Pillar 3 are the Report to Supervisor (RTS) and the public Solvency and Financial Condition Report (SFCR). Both reports are required for each regulated insurance company as well as at an insurance group level.

The Solvency II Directive stipulates that an insurer must publicly produce an annual SFCR. Currently the level of disclosure information varies considerably across the EU. The purpose of the SFCR is to ensure a minimum standard of disclosure, leading to greater transparency not only for policyholders but also for investors, intermediaries, and other interested third parties. This report must be approved by the insurer's management board and should be made available electronically and within four months of an insurer's financial year-end.

The information and format required for the SFCR will be standardized to make it easier for supervisors, policyholders, and third parties to compare one insurer with another and hence achieve the objective of improving market transparency. The report will include:

- A description of the risk exposure, concentration, mitigation, and sensitivity for each risk category.

- Details of the capital management, including the MCR and SCR calculations, plus information on the main differences between the standard formula and any internal models used.

- The basis and methods of valuation for assets and technical provisions, including any significant differences between those used for valuations in financial statements.

- The insurer's performance and governance system.

An additional requirement of the SFCR is that the insurer must certify that the assets have been invested in accordance with the "prudent person" principle. According to the prudent person principle, the complexity of the assets underlying an insurer's portfolio should be commensurate with the ability of the appropriate personnel and systems to understand, monitor, and manage those instruments.

The enhanced disclosure requirements seek to open up the effectiveness and efficiency of risk and capital management to the discipline of market scrutiny. The required disclosure will eventually include any additional capital imposed by the supervisory authority, although this may remain confidential for an interim five-year period following implementation. Supervisors may also allow companies to keep certain information out of the public domain if it could compromise commercial confidentiality or provide undue advantages to its competitors. However, the reason for nondisclosure would have to be publicly explained.

Insurance companies should view the SFCR as a great vehicle to enhance the relationship between them and their customers. A strong capital position and effective risk management can reassure policyholders of the long-term stability of the insurance company and could aid in customer acquisition and retention strategies.

The RTS is a private document and is communicated only to the insurer's appropriate supervisor. The RTS expands on the SFCR's disclosures using a similar, prescribed structure, but this time presenting the information differently as part of the ongoing supervisory dialogue with the insurer. The frequency with which an insurance company has to provide full qualitative information through the RTS will be linked to the intensity of the SRP. The Solvency II Directive states that the RTS must be produced every five years, at minimum, but at supervisory discretion the frequency may be increased up to an annual basis.

The RTS requires information relating to these example areas that are not required in the SFCR:

- Business and risk strategies, including the insurer's continuity plan
- Legal and regulatory issues affecting the insurer
- Variance against plan rather than prior reporting period
- Future anticipated solvency needs, underwriting performance projections, and changes in risk exposure

▦ Significant additional disclosure explaining the results of the internal models

CONCLUSION

Although Solvency II's impact is likely to vary from company to company and from country to country, it has the potential to bring huge improvements to the insurance industry. It will provide a level playing field by ensuring consistent regulation across Europe. It should also improve the solvency of the industry, and that means better protection for consumers.

In addition, best practices in risk management have developed rapidly in recent years. Solvency II will provide incentives to encourage the insurance industry to adopt these practices. It will also enable competitive advantage in the global insurance market place by allowing insurance companies the freedom to choose their own risk profile, as long as they hold adequate capital. More efficient capital allocation leads to lower prices for consumers, while a lower risk of company failure leads to greater confidence in the industry and financial stability.

The scope of Solvency II is restricted to insurers conducting business in the EU, but its success may have greater implications globally, as a number of other national regulators, including those in Japan, are reviewing the regulations with a view to introducing similar risk-based capital regulations. Finally, if Solvency II is properly executed, it has the ability to fulfill its objective of providing solidity to the volatile financial services industry.

The proposed date for implementation of Solvency II is January 1, 2013. This will present many challenges not only to the insurance industry but also to the member states that must bring into force the laws, regulations, and administrative provisions necessary to comply with Solvency II by this time. According to a European Commission Solvency II Assessment conducted in October 2007, "the initial cost of implementing Solvency II for the whole EU insurance industry will be €2–3 billion. However these costs will be outweighed in the long run by the expected benefits."[8]

According to Thomas Steffen, chairman of CEIOPS at the time the Level 1 Solvency II text was published, "Solvency II is not just about capital. It is a change of behavior."[9] Insurance companies that view Solvency II as just another regulatory requirement will be at a competitive disadvantage to those that embrace the directive to improve their business and long-term future.

The Economic Balance Sheet

TOTAL BALANCE SHEET APPROACH

The preceding chapters have emphasized that Solvency II is principles-based rather than rules-based. The underlying philosophy that drives regulatory change and the construction of regulation has experienced massive upheaval recently. There has been a move by regulators away from the Basel II–type approach, which, although still allowing internal modeling of underlying risk parameters, is almost entirely rules-based on the level of aggregation of risk type and divisional risk, to a far more principles-based approach. Whether this ushers in a new world order as far as regulation is concerned has yet to be seen, but at a minimum it is necessary to recognize that the underlying regulatory frameworks of Basel II and Solvency I are quite distinct from the principles-based departure point of Solvency II.

One could argue that a rules-based approach might be viewed as relatively simplistic compared to a principles-based approach, where each regulated entity may have its own interpretation of a set of principles. From a regulator's perspective, the regulations, even under a rules-based system, are already extremely complex and sophisticated.

Assessing the stringency with which institutions have implemented their particular interpretation of the rules requires highly educated individuals working within the regulatory environments of each country. Generally speaking, Basel II rules have been relatively explicit in terms of interpretation. Where clarification has been required, position papers have been made available by the Bank for International Settlements, the institution mandated to facilitate international monetary and financial cooperation and serve as the bank to central banks; it is expected that clarification of a principles-based approach will be far harder, given the scope for somewhat broader interpretations.

It is likely that the choice of a principles-based framework by the European Commission will lead to more sophisticated and more expensive regulation. It has been argued, however, that while the capital requirements under the Solvency I framework have been relatively more easily calculated, the disadvantage is that the calculated capital requirement is rarely, if ever, aligned to the true risk profile of the institution, and moreover may incentivize regulatory arbitrage, ultimately degrading the degree of policyholder protection. The benefits of overcoming these disadvantages are perceived as far outweighing the difficulties in implementing and regulating a principles-based approach.

The European Commission instituted the key Solvency II principles of the three-pillar structure, risk-based supervision, and fair value, precisely because of the apparent weaknesses of the Solvency I Directive. Solvency I is an accounting approach that limits recognition of diversification and risk mitigation, applies at a single company level, contains limited risk governance and risk disclosure requirements, and moreover is based on simplistic formulae that may create perverse incentives in capital requirements. The presumed payoff of a more sophisticated and more expensive principles-based approach is transparency in the institution's risk exposure and a better recognition of the benefits of risk diversification and risk mitigation.

Fundamental to the principles-based solvency framework is the adoption of the economic balance sheet, also known as the total balance sheet approach or solvency balance sheet. The total balance sheet integrates all risk types within the required solvency capital calculation from a policyholder's perspective. In other words, policyholders are comforted knowing that policyholder protection exists in the form of available capital, known as own funds in Solvency II, which represent the difference between the market-consistent value of assets (MVA) and liabilities (MVL). *Market-consistent valuation* means that assets and liabilities are marked to market or marked to model to reflect economic value rather than accounting value.[1] To maintain an adequate solvency coverage ratio of the total balance sheet, loss-absorbing components of available own funds, defined as "eligible own funds" in Solvency II, must be greater than the solvency capital requirement (SCR).

At this point one should see the SCR as being a currency-denominated value representing a capital requirement based on a worst-case scenario. The SCR is determined by means of the integration of all asset and liability risks and the impact of changes in value of assets and liabilities on the overall solvency of an insurance entity. Aggregation of the effects of these risks in the SCR calculation should take account of different lines of business as well as different risk types impacting an insurer. In the event that the ratio of eligible own funds to SCR falls below 1, a supervisory ladder of intervention is triggered, the lowest rung of which is the minimum capital requirement (MCR). The MCR is the point at which the supervisor would seek the recapitalization or run-off of the insurance entity.

In fact, the classification by risk type and line of business has been harmonized by CEIOPS in the standard formula, in effect establishing a typology for the insurance industry. There are five main risk modules, each of which, with the exception of default risk, has in turn its own risk submodules. These high-level risk modules are:

1. Non-life underwriting risk
2. Life underwriting risk
3. Health underwriting risk
4. Market risk
5. Default risk

Aggregation takes account of diversification benefits between risk modules, between lines of business, and with recognition of risk mitigation techniques.

In fact, the total balance sheet is not a great diversion from the rules that govern International Financial Reporting Standards (IFRS), which insist on calculating the apparently "true" value of assets and liabilities based on their tradability and fungibility within the market as a whole. The divergence of value in market instruments and capital instruments from book values can be enormous. The last decade has seen a move throughout the world of accounting toward an IFRS approach, and now also in the Solvency II Directive. This requires that the true market value of a bond or any capital instrument be calculated using appropriate interest rates and appropriate current market information rather than book value.

Likewise, for the liabilities of an insurance or reinsurance company, the "true" economic market value should be calculated in order to derive the true net asset value, which is the difference between assets and liabilities. However, the liabilities of an insurance company include not only the capital market liabilities that may have been incurred but also the insurance liabilities of paying out policyholders as claims and benefits fall due. The heterogeneity in insurance products implies the lack of a robust secondary market in any particular liability type. As such, determination of the tradability, fungibility, and overall valuation of these liabilities in the true economic sense is far more difficult than in a mark-to-market scenario.

For capital market instruments that can be marked to market, a market-consistent valuation approach for liabilities on the insurance entity's balance sheet is appropriate, in the same way that it would be appropriate for the market-consistent valuation of assets. However, in order to calculate the so-called market value of liabilities for liabilities that are not capital market instruments and are therefore not particularly well, if at all tradable, a different approach is required. Here CEIOPS distinguishes between capital market instruments that are traded and those that are really policyholder liabilities on the book of an insurer, using the concept of hedgeability. In other words, CEIOPS defines hedgeable instruments to be those that can be valued using market-consistent valuation; nonhedgeable instruments (i.e., policyholder obligations) are valued using the linear addition of the best estimate of the liabilities plus a risk margin.

Market value of policyholder liabilities is determined by the technical provisions, which are the liabilities recognized on the balance sheet to meet insurance obligations. Technical provisions are calculated as a best estimate, which corresponds to the probability weighted average of the expected value of discounted cash flows, plus a risk margin, being the cost of capital to a third party of assuming the liabilities in the event of run-off. All cash flows that are expected to be required to cover the liabilities as they mature, based on actuarial assumptions, must be included in this calculation.

CEIOPS includes what can be seen as a margin of error on the best estimate in the form of the risk margin. In recognizing the possibility that an insurance company might find itself in a distressed scenario, just prior to failure it would experience severe difficulty in trading out or selling its insurance liabilities to a third-party white knight. It is therefore required that the inherent risks in a distressed situation attract an additional consideration. The purpose of the risk margin is effectively to cover the cost of capital that would be incurred by a third party in purchasing the liabilities from a distressed insurer in run-off.

A minimum of 600 basis points (bps) has been proposed as a temporary placeholder for the cost of capital rate, on the assumption that this provides adequate assurance that the value of technical provisions would be sufficient if the insurer were to transfer its rights and obligations to another undertaking, even under a stressed scenario. This amount is probably too low when one considers that credit default swap spreads on AAA-rated debt of certain banks during the 2008–2009 crisis reached as much as a 1,000 bps.[2] Although 600 bps is likely sufficient prudence under most conditions, one could hypothesize scenarios where it may prove inadequate, particularly if the assessed capital base to which the rate is applied has been systematically underestimated.

The calculations of both the MVA and the MVL—the latter comprising the market-consistent value of capital instruments and also the best estimate of liabilities plus risk margin for nonhedgeable liabilities—will result in a positive net asset value of a solvent insurer. CEIOPS refers to this net asset value as available own funds. In other words, available own funds are simply the MVA less the MVL.

In a world subject to volatility, own funds must be recognized as prone to volatility, given that changes in market conditions result in changes to the MVA and MVL. One should therefore recognize own funds as being themselves stochastic. It is possible under different economic scenarios to calculate a distribution of possible own funds value over a one-year horizon at the prescribed confidence level of 99.5 percent. This concept is derived from the value at risk (VaR) methodology introduced by J. P. Morgan and made freely available in 1994. The VaR method instantly received wide acclaim and was popularly adopted, being institutionalized in the 1996 amendment to Basel I for the calculation of market risk.[3]

VaR can be defined as the worst loss that may be expected with a certain probability over a specific horizon from a fixed (static) set of positions. It is based on the frequency distribution of possible outcomes for own funds. A portfolio with a VaR of $1 million at the 99.5 percent confidence level can be expected to realize losses greater than $1 million once in every 200 years. VaR is therefore not the worst possible loss. On one hand, as a probabilistic statement of the potential change in portfolio value given an extreme event, VaR cannot answer the question of how much could be lost. On the other hand, as an indicator of the required regulatory and economic capital cushions necessary to support a portfolio, VaR is a valuable tool.

VaR enjoys a particular advantage in that it can be applied to any roll-up level: at financial instrument level, by line of business, or by risk modules. Once the specific risk factors contributing to the volatility of a portfolio of assets or liabilities have been identified, the future distribution of portfolio value can be derived at the chosen horizon, using one of three alternatives:

1. An analytical parametric method, such as variance-covariance or extreme value theory
2. A historic simulation method
3. A Monte Carlo simulation method[4]

The easiest VaR method to implement is the *variance-covariance* or *delta-normal* parametric method commonly used for market risk, which assumes that holding period returns are normally distributed.

Because the normal distribution is completely described by the first two moments of the distribution, the mean and variance, a straightforward formula for the mean and variance of the portfolio return distribution can be derived from the multivariate normal risk factor distribution and the portfolio composition. As a result, the analytical approach is the simplest and most easily estimated VaR measure.

Historical simulation VaR differs from the analytical approach by not necessitating the use of analytical distributions. Here the VaR is estimated using the empirical loss or profit and loss distributions, preferably calibrated over a period of some years of historical data, substituting the assumption of normality with the assumption that the near future will be similar to the past. This calculation is easily performed by repricing one's current portfolio of assets and liabilities as if this portfolio were held throughout past history. In attempting to apply this theory to the insurance market, one has to recognize that while it may work very well for the asset side of the balance sheet, it is unlikely to work well for the liabilities side, since it necessitates the historical repricing of both hedgeable and nonhedgeable liabilities.

Due to analytical and historical VaR's inherent shortcomings, many portfolios will of necessity require more computationally intensive Monte Carlo VaR simulation. Historical simulation VaR may be inappropriate because of the uncertainty surrounding the representativeness of the data period. Many risks do not accommodate analytical approaches because, for example, their distributions exhibit discontinuous "jump" stochastic processes or fat tails. Risks can also be very difficult to parameterize and calibrate because of insufficient data points. Payoffs to portfolios comprising diverse instruments, particularly those instruments containing options, may preclude analytical solutions. In such instances, Monte Carlo's reliability tends to trump its complexity and computational intensity.

The workhorse of quantitative risk management is undoubtedly the random (stochastic) Monte Carlo simulation technique. Monte Carlo simulation models are a class of algorithm relying on repeated random sampling to compute the most likely stochastic outcome of phenomena subject to significant input uncertainty. Monte Carlo simulation imitates real-life systems by repeated iteration. As many as 100,000 simulations may be run, creating a probability distribution for each underlying risk factor of 100,000 scenarios. The multitude of scenarios is often necessary to capture the strong hysteresis or path-dependency effects that many real-life economic systems exhibit, by which minor changes in initial conditions may result in extremely diverse outcomes. For example, an increase in asset volatility coupled with an exogenous economic shock may increase the future costs of guarantees on investment products significantly, even if the probability of such an event is low. Monte Carlo simulation is a reliable way of creating such path-dependent scenario distributions.

Whichever method is used, one envisages a range of possible outcomes for own funds, where the left tail of the distribution represents the rare case where own funds would be under severe pressure, calibrated under Solvency II to a risk of ruin probability of 1 in 200 years; the right tail represents perfectly benign market conditions; and the mean of the distribution represents more typical conditions. At this stage one has simulated the volatility of own funds, which allows one to calculate the stipulated VaR of own funds. This volatility of own funds, whose value can be distributed under different market conditions, is in fact the solvency capital ratio, the 99.5 percent tail event over a one-year horizon of available own funds.[5]

Chapter VI of the final text of the Solvency II Directive stipulates the quantitative requirements underpinning the total balance sheet approach in six sections:

1. Valuation of assets and liabilities
2. Technical provisions
3. Own funds
4. SCR
5. MCR
6. Investment rules

The next section briefly summarizes the salient implications of these quantitative requirements before discussing the determination of the SCR in the context of the standard formula. The possible implications to an insurer of the standard formula are considered as an incentive to adopt the internal models approach. Internal models are the subject of Chapter 7. Whichever approach is used, the SCR is a coverage ratio of eligible own funds to SCR greater than 1.

QUANTITATIVE STIPULATIONS OF THE LEVEL 1 TEXT

At this juncture it is necessary to define the SCR more comprehensively. For the sake of clarity, many of the concepts introduced in the previous section are looked at in greater depth. The SCR is the crux of the Solvency II framework, the construction and aggregation of which is supported by the quantitative stipulations for the creation of an economic balance sheet. The SCR should be calibrated so as to ensure that all quantifiable risks to which the insurer is exposed are taken into account, including all new business expected to be written over the following year. It should correspond to the VaR of the basic own funds at a confidence level of 99.5 percent over one year. In other words, the risk of ruin—the probability of the total loss exceeding the capital requirement—may not be more than 0.5 percent. It is worth reiterating that aggregation of the SCR should take account of the benefits of risk diversification and risk mitigation techniques and include at least the following five risk modules:

1. Non-life underwriting risk
2. Life underwriting risk
3. Health underwriting risk
4. Market risk
5. Default risk

The Level 1 text specifies that assets and liabilities should be valued "at the amount for which they could be exchanged between knowledgeable willing parties in an arm's length transaction." Unbiased valuation of assets and liabilities is the cornerstone of the total balance sheet approach and economic risk-based supervision. CEIOPS's Level 2 advice recommends the adoption of IFRS fair value as a reference point for building a coherent balance sheet consistent with the economic valuation principles of Solvency II.[6] This should not interfere with the use of local generally accepted accounting principles for general-purpose financial statements.

As emphasized earlier, fair value of assets is determined by mark to market wherever possible. When not possible, assets are marked to model, provided justifiable model assumptions can be provided to the supervisor. Hedgeable liabilities are similarly marked to market, while nonhedgeable liabilities are calculated as the best estimate plus a risk margin.

Market-consistent valuation of regularly traded plain vanilla financial instruments is simply their observed market value. At the other end of the complexity spectrum, assets and liabilities having market-contingent benefits may require complex market-consistent stochastic Monte Carlo simulation methods. In between are financial instruments with no optionality, for which deterministic projections may be used, and instruments with simple optionality, such as puts and calls, for which closed form solutions may be employed.

Given that market-consistent values of insurance liabilities are in general unobservable in the market, the market value of the technical provision for a nonhedgeable risk is derived from the best estimate plus a risk margin. Best estimate of a liability is calculated as the probability weighted average of expected future cash flows, discounted at the risk-free rate using AAA-rated government bonds as the reference rate for the interest rate term structure. Risk margin is the cost of capital of own funds equivalent to the SCR needed to support an underwriting obligation over its lifetime, which can also be seen as the economic cost of underwriting the risk. Risk margin is determined using a cost of capital approach, assumed in quantitative impact study 4 (QIS 4) to be 6 percent.

The best estimate is calculated net of any deductions that may arise from reinsurance and special-purpose vehicles. It includes all future payments to policyholders and beneficiaries, all future expenses, and claims and expenses inflation. Realistic assumptions must be made regarding optionality embedded within policies.

Technical provisions may also be calculated as a whole rather than as a best estimate plus a risk margin. This would occur when liability obligations may be reliably estimated with reference to a replicating portfolio of financial assets for which a market value is available. The replicating portfolio is a pool of assets that closely mirrors the characteristics of the liabilities. No explicit risk margin is incorporated into this calculation, since the costs of hedging the liabilities, such as transaction costs and unexpected losses, are fully reflected by the market value of the instruments that comprise the replicating portfolio.

Whether technical provisions are calculated as best estimate plus risk margin or as a whole, the basic premise is that those provisions are sufficient to transfer obligations to another insurer in the event of run-off. It is assumed that the liabilities are transferred to a reference undertaking, which is a shell that has no prior obligations or own funds. After transfer, this hypothetical entity should have own funds equal to the SCR needed to support those obligations. Because CEIOPS assumes that run-off is in practice likely feasible only by line of business, segmentation for the purpose of calculating the reference undertaking SCR is by line of business.[7] Thus no diversification benefit can exist between lines of business in the risk margin calculation.

The capital resources or available own funds that are required to support the SCR are subject to eligibility criteria. In addition to the fundamental criterion that eligible own funds be held to support the SCR at a 99.5 percent VaR over one year, minimum levels of own funds that should be held to cover the SCR and the MCR are specified, based on their quality. To effect this, own funds are categorized in three tiers, based on their eligibility to cover the SCR. Eligibility is met according to six criteria, with criterion 2 being the most important:

1. The degree of subordination of the instrument
2. Full capacity to absorb losses on a going concern basis and in run-off
3. Permanence or sufficient duration
4. Freedom from requirements such as interest or dividend payments and refunding incentives
5. Absence of fixed charges
6. No other encumbrances

In understanding how the mix and quality of available own funds is seen to define the quality of the capital structure, it is also necessary to differentiate between basic own funds and ancillary own funds. Table 6.1 summarizes own funds criteria.

Table 6.1 Own Funds Criteria

Tier	Basic Own Funds	Ancillary Own Funds	SCR Coverage	MCR Coverage
1	Criteria 1–6	Not available	>50%	80%
2	Criteria 1, 3–6	Criteria 1–6	<Tier 1	>20%
3	Other	Other	<15%	Not available

CEIOPS defines *basic own funds* as comprised of the excess of the MVA over MVL, plus subordinated liabilities. Basic own funds that can absorb losses completely are included in Tier 1; basic own funds that cannot fully absorb losses, but that otherwise satisfy the eligibility criteria, are included in Tier 2. All other basic own funds are designated Tier 3.

Ancillary own funds are callable capital instruments that do not qualify as basic own funds and hence are ineligible for inclusion in Tier 1. Examples include callable capital instruments and letters of credit or guarantees held in trust for the benefit of insurance creditors. Since ancillary funds are callable instruments, they nevertheless may be used to replenish the level of basic own funds, as required, and hence are available to cover the SCR but not the MCR.

The inherent volatility of own funds, whose value can be distributed under different market conditions, is in fact the solvency capital ratio, the 99.5 percent tail event over a one-year horizon of own funds. Within the SCR, the VaR is calculated per risk module but is integrated from a diversification perspective using predefined covariance matrices and assumption sets and parameter values provided by CEIOPS for the standard formula. However, one can also use an internal model for the integration of these risk modules.

Broad principles govern the calculation of SCR at a risk module level and the aggregation of the different SCRs into the overall insurance entity's SCR.[8] However, the insurance entity is required to indicate whether it will be adopting the standard formula or the full or partial internal models approach. Under the standard formula, the

SCR is calculated as the sum of the basic solvency capital requirement, the capital requirement for operational risk, and an adjustment for the loss-absorbing capacity of technical provisions and deferred taxes. The standard formula approach uses a standard predefined correlation matrix for the basic SCR aggregation.[9]

Insurers wishing to adopt the more sophisticated full or partial internal models approach will use their own assessments to determine a correlation matrix or use other methodologies, such as copula functions, which match their data and outcomes to aggregate and diversify across the SCRs of different risks. CEIOPS has not left the question of risk aggregation and the benefits of diversification entirely in the hands of insurers, but has stipulated a set of principles that must be adhered to which govern the decision the insurer will take in terms of risk aggregation and diversification.

Internal models may be employed partially to calculate one or more of the risk modules, the capital requirement for operational risk, and the adjustment for the loss-absorbing capacity of technical provisions and deferred taxes. Insurers must justify use of such partial models rather than the full internal model approach, and the partial models must be able to be integrated into the SCR standard formula. Significant changes to partial or full internal models require supervisory approval.

The MCR is a lower bound of eligible own funds beneath which policyholders and beneficiaries are deemed to be exposed to an unacceptable level of risk, triggering final supervisory intervention. It is calibrated to the VaR of basic own funds at a confidence level of 85 percent over one year.

MCR is calculated as a function of technical provisions, written premiums, capital at risk, deferred taxes, and administrative expenses. A corridor is prescribed for the MCR, which should total at least 25 percent, but no more than 45 percent, of the SCR. In addition, nonlife insurers must comply with a minimum capital requirement of €2.2 million, and life insurers and reinsurers, of €3.2 million.

This linear formulation of the MCR is akin to the current solvency rules and hence is not properly risk-based.[10] The reasons often cited for the MCR not being risk-based are easily calculable lower rungs on the ladder of intervention and enhanced capacity on the part of insurers and supervisors alike for timely awareness of an emerging untenable capital position.

CEIOPS has specified the actual constitution of own funds in the SCR and MCR formulations and in the constitution of the MCR corridor in order to prevent a simultaneous breach of SCR and MCR and hence to ensure a workable supervisory ladder of intervention. The proportion of Tier 1 own funds available to cover the SCR is required to be greater than 50 percent of the total amount of eligible own funds needed, while the proportion of Tier 3 own funds should be less than 15 percent. It must be remembered that Tier 3 own funds are not deemed of sufficient quality to cover the MCR. Given the corridor for MCR of between 25 and 45 percent of SCR, CEIOPS has advised that Tier 1 own funds should be 80 percent of the MCR, which would still allow a sufficient ladder of intervention, rather than 100 percent, which would result in simultaneous breach.

The sixth stipulation from Chapter VI of the Solvency II Directive simply lays down the principles that should be adhered to for responsible investing. All investments should be undertaken in accordance with the prudent person principle. Furthermore, assets held to cover the SCR and MCR should be invested with regard to the security, quality, liquidity, and profitability of the portfolio. Assets held to cover technical provisions should be appropriate to the nature and duration of the insurance liabilities. Investments should be diversified and not expose the insurer to undue risk concentration. Given the role played by mortgage-backed securities and collateralized debt obligations in the financial crisis, it is hardly surprising that CEIOPS has specified that insurers may invest in asset-backed securities only if the originator retains more than 5 percent of the economic exposure.

THE STANDARD FORMULA

The standard formula uses a prescribed correlation matrix to aggregate risk modules to derive the SCR. It is a bottom-up approach, meaning that each individual risk is first evaluated in isolation. To derive the basic solvency capital requirement (BSCR), solvency capital requirements must be quantified for the five basic risk modules:

1. Non-life underwriting risk

2. Life underwriting risk

3. Health underwriting risk

4. Market risk

5. Default risk

The basic risk modules are comprised of several risk submodules, as shown in Figure 6.1, which is CEIOPS's aggregation diagram. Table 6.2 labels this diagram. The capital requirement is calculated for each risk submodule before being aggregated into the larger risk module capital requirement, incorporating the dependency structure between submodules, including by line of business for underwriting risks.

Aggregation by module to a total risk capital requirement for the BSCR requires that a dependency structure between all risk submodules is in place in order to realize the benefits of portfolio diversification. Diversification benefits were first introduced into financial thinking by Harry Markowitz, who demonstrated the existence of an efficient frontier of portfolio diversification,[11] making extensive use of

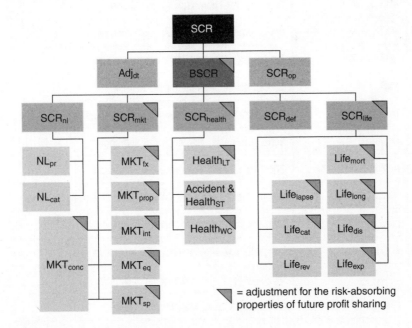

Figure 6.1 SCR Aggregation. Copyright © CEIOPS 2008.

Table 6.2 SCR Modules

Adj_{dt}	Adjustment for the risk-absorbing properties of future profit-sharing module
BSCR	Basic SCR module
SCR_{op}	SCR module for operational risk
SCR_{nl}	SCR module for non-life insurance risk
SCR_{mkt}	SCR module for market risk
SCR_{health}	SCR module for health insurance risk
SCR_{def}	SCR module for default risk
SCR_{life}	SCR module for life insurance
NL_{pr}	Premium and reserve risk submodule for non-life risk
NL_{cat}	Catastrophe risk submodule for non-life risk
MKT_{fx}	Foreign exchange risk submodule for market risk
MKT_{prop}	Property risk submodule for market risk
MKT_{int}	Interest rate risk submodule for market risk
MKT_{eq}	Equity risk submodule for market risk
MKT_{sp}	Spread risk submodule for market risk
MKT_{conc}	Concentration risk submodule for market risk
$Health_{LT}$	Long-term health insurance risk submodule
$Accident \& Health_{ST}$	Short-term health insurance risk submodule
$Health_{WC}$	Worker's compensation risk submodule for health insurance
$Life_{mort}$	Mortality risk submodule for life insurance
$Life_{long}$	Longevity risk submodule for life insurance
$Life_{dis}$	Disability risk submodule for life insurance
$Life_{exp}$	Expense risk submodule for life insurance
$Life_{lapse}$	Lapse risk submodule for life insurance

Table 6.2 SCR Modules (continued)

Life$_{cat}$	Catastrophe risk submodule for life insurance
Life$_{rev}$	Revision risk submodule for life insurance

a 1900 paper by Louis Bachelier.[12] This concept has been adopted in the so-called economic capital approach employed by banks and large corporations throughout the world. It is based on the principle that there is a less-than-1 correlation between different risks within the same line of business or the same type of risk within different lines of business. Imperfect correlation between risks implies a diversification benefit, whereby the sum of individual capital requirements is greater than the capital requirement as a whole, which takes the diversification benefit between individual components into account.

The total balance sheet approach of Solvency II allows for such diversification benefits. In general, mutually independent lines of business will take a correlation coefficient of 0 while the supervisory authority will stipulate a coefficient closer to 1 for submodules with strong dependency. The correlation matrix for aggregation to the BSCR is prescribed by the directive, whereas insurers using the internal models approach will wish to achieve greater recognition of diversification effects.

Operational risk capital enjoys no diversification benefit within the modular structure; it is calculated separately and added to the BSCR. The operational risk capital charge is calculated as the lower of 30 percent of the basic SCR, or 3 percent of premium plus 0.3 percent of reserves. Summation to the SCR requires incorporating the adjustment for the loss-absorbing capacity of technical provisions and deferred taxes into the SCR.

The manner in which all of these risk modules are treated is reasonably complex. For example, a non-life insurer would need to calculate the SCR for the non-life module, market risk module, and default risk module and aggregate these for the BSCR. The next sections provide a more detailed view of the underlying standard formula risk calculations for a non-life insurer. Please note throughout that an insurer will be making use of coefficient values and predetermined factor values in a number of calculations, where those coefficients and factors have been stipulated under the standard formula by CEIOPS. CEIOPS has arrived at these coefficients and factors in order to make it easier to calculate the SCR. However, obviously a compromise exists between using the standardized approach and using possibly more accurate internal models. It becomes apparent when analyzing these factors that many have been determined in a reasonably empirical manner, whereas others have been determined more qualitatively. It is important to note that these predetermined values of parameters used in the SCR and MCR calculations are precisely the ones that can be addressed more carefully in the implementation of an internal models approach.

NON-LIFE UNDERWRITING RISK MODULE

This section covers the treatment of the non-life underwriting risk module under the standardized approach. Non-life risk is comprised of the premium and reserve underwriting risk submodule and the catastrophe risk submodule. Premium risk arises in the event that claims are more frequent and/or more severe than expected, so that premiums are insufficient to cover actual losses. Reserve risk is the risk that additional technical provisions may have to be raised against previous years' claims. The premium and reserve risk submodule takes account of diversification by line of business and implicitly of geographical diversification. Since the SCR parameters are calibrated using the historic volatility of the whole business of an average representative undertaking (i.e. the average insurance entity), these parameters already reflect an average level of geographical diversification. The catastrophe risk submodule reflects the effect of extreme events on claims expenses in premium and reserve risk. It is assumed that there is a correlation of 0 between the premium and reserve risk submodule and the catastrophe risk submodule.

Capital required for the premium and reserve risk submodule is determined by a factor model, in which predetermined standard deviation values are multiplied by the insurer's premiums written and reserves created. The model is created in two stages.

Stage 1 determines separate volume and standard deviation measures for premium and reserve risk for each line of business. Market-wide estimates for the standard deviation of premium and reserve risk are specified in CEIOPS's Consultation Paper 71, "SCR Standard Formula—Calibration of Non-Life Underwriting Risk." CEIOPS's calibration of the input factors to the calculation already allows for an average level of geographical diversification. Under the standard formula, no further geographic diversification benefit would be allowed.

Stage 2 derives a combined standard deviation weighted by line of business volume for premium and reserve risk by aggregating the standard deviations and volumes from stage 1 using a correlation between premium and reserve risk of 50 percent. The capital requirement for premium and reserve risk is calculated using the total volume from stage 1 and a function of the overall standard deviation, determined using a line of business correlation matrix provided by CEIOPS.

The premium and reserve risk submodule is calibrated to take account only of regularly occurring losses, excluding losses occurring as a result of extreme events. The risk of events with extreme uncertainty is evaluated separately in the catastrophe risk submodule, typically using a standard scenario-based approach developed by CEIOPS. In addition to the standard scenario-based approach, under QIS 4 a factor-based alternative proportional to net written premiums could be used if the standardized approach is not relevant to the specific circumstances of the insurer. It is likely that the actual determination of standardized catastrophe scenarios and their aggregation will be subject to significant national discretion.

MARKET RISK MODULE

This section discusses the determination of the market risk submodule result under the standardized approach. Market risk is the risk of losses on investments or the failure to generate sufficient returns on those investments. It is comprised of six submodules:

1. Foreign exchange risk
2. Property risk
3. Interest rate risk
4. Equity risk
5. Spread risk
6. Concentration risk

The foreign exchange risk submodule uses a scenario-based approach to calculate currency risk, which is a maximum change up or down of 25 percent, at the 99.5 percentile and the 0.5 percentile respectively. The calibration of the scenario is based on the distribution of holding period rate of returns on 14 currency pairs against the euro and the British pound, including a currency portfolio that is a proxy for emerging markets.

The property risk capital charge is based on a net asset value change in property values following a predefined stress scenario. The stress applied to all property types is a 25 percent fall in value, calibrated on the Industrial Property Databank time series of United Kingdom total return indices.

The interest rate risk submodule captures the effect of a change in the interest rate term structure, or change in the volatility of interest rates, on the combined value of assets and liabilities. The interest rate specific capital requirement is determined using two stress scenarios, of one upward and one downward shock, at each maturity of the term structure using euro and British pound zero-coupon bonds and euro and British pound London Interbank offered rate (LIBOR) rates. The collection of annual percentage rate changes has been extracted by CEIOPS using principal component analysis of the variance-covariance structure of the underlying data. Four principal components representing the level, slope, curvature, and twist of the yield curve, accounting for 99.98 percent of the variability in the annual percentage rate change, were fed into a regression model to derive the stressed rates at each maturity level at a 99.5 percent confidence level. The capital charge is subsequently the maximum of the capital charges for the upward and downward shocks, subject to a minimum of 0.

In comparing the property and interest rate submodules, it is evident that the property risk submodule is an instance in which there is an opportunity for insurers to calculate a more accurate internal model. Because the work performed by CEIOPS in calibrating the interest rate risk submodule is likely to be far more accurate than the methodology employed in the property risk submodule, any gains in implementing an internal model for the interest rate risk submodule would be far less significant.

Equity risk represents the combined effect of a stress on equity values and a change in equity volatility on the market value of assets and liabilities. A stress of 45 percent is proposed for global equities and 55 percent for "other" equities—emerging market equity, private equity, hedge funds, and commodities. The correlation assumed by CEIOPS between these two equity classifications is 75 percent. The higher stress for other equities reflects the greater volatility observed in the other equity category through statistical analysis. Firms are also required to assess whether they are affected by equity volatility risk.

Spread risk is the risk that an investment will suffer a capital loss as the result of a change in the credit spread of that instrument over the risk-free interest rate. A change in market value of bonds, structured products, or credit derivatives will follow a change in the spread between risk-free and risk-bearing investments. The capital charge is determined by means of a factor-based calculation that considers a rise in credit spreads. This factor is a function of the rating class of the exposure, which is calibrated to deliver a shock consistent with VaR at 99.5 percent confidence. This method does not explicitly model migration and default risk, which is implicit in the calibrated factor.

Concentration risk is applicable to assets considered in the property risk, interest rate risk, equity risk, and spread risk submodules within the market risk module but excludes assets covered by the counterparty default risk module. Concentration risk is assessed based on the market value of capital investments by counterparty rating. For an individual counterparty rated A or above, its fixed interest and equity securities may not exceed 3 percent of the insurer's total assets. Counterparties rated below A may not exceed 1.5 percent of total assets. Concentration in an exposure to a particular entity, or "name," above these thresholds attracts a capital charge determined by a factor based on the credit rating.

DEFAULT RISK MODULE

In addition to the underwriting risk submodules and the market risk submodule, aggregation to the BSCR under the standardized approach requires the estimation of a default risk submodule. Default risk is the risk of experiencing an unexpected loss on a credit obligation, based on the failure of that credit obligation or rating downgrade of the counterparty.

Exposures are distinguished as being type 1 or type 2. Type 1 exposures are those that are likely to be rated, such as bank and reinsurance counterparties. The capital requirement for these counterparties is determined based on their probability of default (PD) and the probable loss given that a default occurs (LGD), where the PD is derived either from the external rating or from the solvency ratio rating of an insurer or reinsurer. The capital requirement for counterparty default risk of type 2 exposures of unrated counterparties under the standardized approach uses a simple factor-based approach. The total SCR for the default risk module is derived by means of a square root formula of the capital requirements for type 1 and type 2 exposures.

CONCLUSION

The total balance sheet approach is a decisive move away from simplistic capital requirements in the direction of a more risk-sensitive capital regime, with the overarching principle of policyholder protection at its core. This economic or solvency balance sheet approach integrates all risk types within the SCR calculation on a fair value basis. The calculation of SCR corresponds to the VaR of the insurer's own funds available to absorb losses at a confidence level of 99.5 percent over one year.

In the standard formula approach to Solvency II, the basic solvency capital requirement is comprised of three underwriting risk modules—life, non-life, and health products—and one risk module each for market risk and default risk. The results are then aggregated by means of a predefined correlation matrix. To this result is added the solvency capital requirement for operational risk and an adjustment for future profit sharing to give the total SCR.

CEIOPS has calibrated the input stresses and factors for the calculation of individual risk submodule capital requirements across the insurance industry as a whole in order to provide the standardized approach. An internal impact analysis will provide each individual insurer with examples of areas in which internal modeling would be of benefit. It is only natural, therefore, that many insurers will wish to employ the internal models approach to develop a more nuanced view of the risks inherent within their portfolios, despite the considerable effort and expense of doing so.

As illustrated for non-life underwriting risk, market risk, and default risk, the calculation at an individual risk module level and the calculation process for the aggregation of risk modules, although predetermined under the standardized approach, require substantial and accurate counterparty exposure data and historical internal data. The calculation and aggregation of risk modules require considerable precision from insurers even under the standardized approach, but internal modeling can be implemented in particular submodules where the benefits are greater than others.

CHAPTER **7**

Internal Models

COMPLEXITY OF IMPLEMENTATION

Internal models form the heart and soul of the underlying motivation for Solvency II. In fact, one could go so far as to say that an organization that wishes to embark on Solvency II but has no intention of moving toward an internal model misses the program's fundamental benefit and advantages. Internal models should be seen as the internally determined parameterization of the underlying risk module models and the quantification of the firm-specific aggregation methods used in the aggregation process of individual risk modules to the total solvency capital requirement (SCR).

It is constructive to compare the internal model concept and process of Solvency II with the implementation of internal models under the Basel II program. Two pertinent, critical differences between the regimes must be noted.

Internal models under the Advanced Internal Ratings–Based (AIRB) approach were for the determination of three key risk parameters on the portfolios of asset classes of the balance sheet: the internal determination of the probabilities of default (PD), exposures at default (EAD), and loss given default (LGD) per obligor or exposure. Solvency II goes further in that internal models can and should be used for both sides of the balance sheet, including both the assets and the liabilities, which are made up of both the hedgeable portion of liabilities, and the nonhedgeable portion of liabilities (the insurance liabilities). In this sense, Solvency II's internal models already cover twice as much ground as Basel II's models.

Another crucial distinction is the fact that even under the AIRB approach, the aggregation of risks in and across different asset classes, as well as the aggregation of different risk types (e.g., credit risk, market risk, and operational risk) was driven by predetermined models. The calibration under AIRB was not calibrated to any particular bank but rather to the universe of banking through the use of the asymptotic single risk factor model (ASRF).[1] It was through this ASRF model that the Basel II risk-weighted asset equation was derived, treating diversification benefits through a single function predetermined by the Basel Committee for Banking Supervision. Solvency II, however, allows insurers to determine their own covariance matrices and other aggregation methods under the internal models approach. These covariance matrices, as well as other, more complex, aggregation methods, can be populated using both quantitative and qualitative methods.

The critical issue for successful Solvency II implementation is that these internal models have to be individually validated through a sophisticated, all-encompassing validation process built into the insurer's overall risk management function. This validation process will be a focal point of supervisory concern. To give an indication of the sheer size of this task, the regulation of less than two dozen banking groups within the United Kingdom covered the majority of U.K. bank assets during the height of the exuberant years prior to 2008 and through the crisis itself. Covering an equivalent percentage of policyholder obligations throughout the United Kingdom would require detailed regulation of more than 100 insurance entities.

The task facing supervisory authorities such as the Financial Services Authority is substantially larger than that faced by authorities under the Basel II regime. A comparison of the relative effort of supervising insurers under Solvency II versus banks under Basel II should be made in the context of three dimensions:

1. There is a larger number of organizations that needs to be regulated.

2. There is increased complexity in the models themselves.

3. The total balance sheet approach under Solvency II involves validation of models across both assets and liabilities, as opposed to assets only under Basel II.

It is worth noting however that amendments being made to Basel II will involve the liability side of the balance sheet going forward, implicit in the new liquidity risk requirements proposed for Basel III.

This chapter illustrates the complexity of constructing, validating, and successfully subjecting these models to the necessary supervisory scrutiny.

DEFINITION AND SCOPE OF INTERNAL MODELS

It is important to note that the Committee of European Insurance and Occupational Pensions Supervisors (CEIOPS) offers no formal definition of what an internal model is. Nor, for that matter, is a formal definition offered as to the scope of what internal models should cover. Remember that a key difference between Solvency II and Basel II is the fact that Solvency II is principles-based whereas Basel II is far more rules-based; this lack of definition is in fact entirely consistent with a principles-based approach. To give an example, it is not necessarily clear whether the concept of internal models, and their validation and regulation, covers the calculation of best estimate for nonhedgeable liabilities.

From one perspective, the best estimate of the nonhedgeable liabilities should not be covered by internal models, since it is a well-understood actuarial process that has been applied for some time. Including the best estimate of liabilities in the scope of what internal models should cover and what should be validated internally and regulated increases complexity and, by implication, the time and effort necessary for implementation and the overall cost associated with regulation.

However, the opposite perspective would hold that, by definition, the SCR ratio is the tail event of a frequency distribution of the net asset value of assets less liabilities, under a vast range of economic scenarios generated by a Economic Scenario Generator tool, which would consistently generate economic scenarios through which the asset pricing and valuation models, and the liability pricing and valuation models, should flow.[2] As such, failure to explicitly include the calculation of best estimate for different classes of liabilities in the scope of internal models *excludes* one of the key pricing functions that are part of the calculation engine for solvency capital.

In Solvency II, unlike Basel II, there is a lack of clarification over this issue of the definition and scope of internal models. The regulatory authorities have purposefully put this issue aside so as not to limit the range of possibilities that they may receive in quantitative impact study applications or in actual preapplications for approval of internal models.

Statements made by regulators in regard to internal models are far clearer regarding what the requirements are from a validation, data, documentation, and precision perspective. This perhaps illustrates the fact that the negative experiences with respect to Basel II implementation and the regulation of its models might well have filtered through to a change in perspective at the outset in terms of Solvency II regulation.

Solvency II specifically states that insurance and reinsurance undertakings may calculate the SCR on the basis of a full or partial internal model. A partial internal model is recognized as one in which certain parts of the portfolio or certain risk modules have been calculated using internal models while others have been calculated using the standard approach. It is possible for an insurer to apply for approval of the partial internal model for specific portfolios, so long as it also validates the total aggregation of risk modules and risk submodules.

INTERNAL MODELS APPLICATION

Supervisors have six months from the date of submission to decide on an insurer's request to use a full or partial internal model. In order for insurers' models to be approved, the companies need to fulfill requirements set out in the Solvency II Directive.[3]

Regulatory authorities have stressed that the main goal of internal models is not a reduction in capital required but better risk management and internal knowledge of the business. They also have stressed, once again likely as a consequence of the Basel II experience, that internal models do not need to be rocket science but should be proportionate to the nature, scale, and complexity of the risks inherent to the business.[4]

The regulators have also stressed that internal models are far more than mathematical models; the key principle underlying internal model approval is the success of the use test. The goal of the use test is to ensure that all internal models are embedded in the running of the business. The importance of the use test cannot be overemphasized. One of the consequences flowing out of the use test is that models cannot simply be black boxes. In this regard, regulators have made it clear that vendor models *cannot* be approved if the calibration and the mathematical process are hidden. Such models therefore must be transparent.

The tests and standards for internal model approval will be set in an integrated, holistic approach. It is extremely important to regulators that insurers be able to demonstrate adequate understanding of the process, use, and results of internal models. In fact, regulators actually intend to interview executives about these models, asking what they are used for, what their scope is, what part of the balance sheet they apply to, and how they are applied in day-to-day decision making.

Regulators will follow a preapplication process, followed by a formal application, followed by an assessment of the application, before a decision will be made. Obviously, the manner in which the preapplication takes place, and the final approval process itself, will be the subject of national discretion. Preapplication should include a policy on model changes, the purpose of which is to satisfy the regulator that future model changes will be within certain boundaries, irrespective of what those boundaries might be. This implies that management needs to determine how the model is likely to evolve in future.

During the assessment phase, supervisors will be interested predominantly in five fundamental requirements regarded by supervisors themselves as essential to embedding an internal model within the undertaking:[5]

1. The scope of the model in terms of what it does and does not cover is regarded as a prerequisite to reconciliation between the modeling framework and the risk management function.

2. The methodology of the model and all submodels must be specified.

3. Full-scale documentation pertaining to all aspects of model development must be compiled.

4. Data quality is regarded as particularly important and is likely to be a focal point for many supervisors. All quantitative and qualitative procedures must be specified and documented.

5. Mapping the technical environment includes the information technology landscape, architecture, and data flow processes.

Insurers must recognize that the requirements regarding data quality, quantitative and qualitative procedures, and the technological environment translate in practice to the need for full audit control and, in particular, full audit management on models, both on the data processes as they pertain to models and on the mathematical and/or qualitative methods as they relate to the process flow of models. Supervisors will assess the desired level of proficiency in attaining and maintaining these processes and procedures. It is expected that supervisors will conduct these assessments through periodic desk-based review and on-site inspection.

The need for high-quality data is absolutely critical, particularly in regard to the use of internal models. As an example, this can be easily appreciated in the context of a Monte Carlo simulation. Whereas previously cost and technology constraints implied analytical reliance on deterministic point estimates, the advent of cheap computing capacity has made the theoretically superior stochastic modeling of financial processes routine. By specifying the behavioral characteristics of the process in terms of underlying functional distributions, conditions are created under which the drudgery of repeated estimations and calculations of variables can be performed by software, culminating in a reliable representation of the probabilities associated with an outcome.

Ideally, the result is a tool capable of rendering great complexity under the constraint of (relatively) few assumptions. Given the integrity of inputs or parameters to the model, the output of a Monte Carlo simulation may reliably estimate a price, a performance, a ranking, or an optimal portfolio composition. The superiority of this method as an estimation technique and its flexibility of application derive from its sensitivity to input parameters, but great care must be taken in the collection of data, specification of functional forms, and relationships between variables.

The most important component of any model will always be reliable, accurate, and consistent data. "Garbage in, garbage out" might be somewhat of a cliché, but the most sophisticated mathematical modeling techniques cannot save a model from data that are inconsistent, erratic, or wrong. The data requirements should not be underestimated. The data will need to be analyzed, cleaned, and stored in a usable format. This is usually the most time-consuming portion of developing simulation engines, especially if engine automation is required for a business process or to qualify as an internal model.

Once the data have been analyzed, cleaned, and stored in a usable format, statistical distributions, historical distributions, parameters, and relationships may be observed and established from the historical data. There are no hard-and-fast rules as to what constitutes a statistically significant data set, but a general rule is that no less than three years' data suffice to derive statistically significant estimates of the distribution functions of variables and the correlations between them. It is preferable to have sufficient data to capture a full economic cycle, but not such a long data series that structural breaks in the data are included that may contradict the assumed economic behavior of the process.

The choice of variables should be informed by the model's purpose and thus should be theoretically identifiable as material to the outcome. Parsimony is not a binding constraint in the construction of a Monte Carlo simulation. In fact, provided the dependency structure between variables is correctly specified, the preferred model would ideally include all relevant variables. The issue is commonly one of the performance perspective versus the predictive perspective. Modeling the

PD on a corporate bond portfolio, for example, might be effected in Excel using just a few of the most discriminatory financial ratios or other obligor characteristics, whereas a full-scale stochastic asset-liability model requires the inclusion of all relevant variables. In the former case, discriminatory variables are selected on the basis of statistical techniques, such as weights of evidence, information values, or stepwise regression. The latter case would include all relevant macroeconomic and microeconomic variables, some of which are chosen statistically (e.g., by logistic regression for behavioral variables), while many of the macro variables would first be subject to time-series analysis and econometric modeling.

The directive allows great freedom of choice when it comes to partial internal models, but insurers must justify why particular risk modules or risk types fall within the scope of partial internal models rather than the standard formula. The individual insurer's arguments may be that a specific categorization of risk for partial models is a better reflection of the risk profile of the undertaking, because of a lack of reliable information to model certain areas. This may be as a result of mergers and acquisitions having taken place, for example. Additionally, the particular insurer's business model needs to be considered insofar as ensuring that the complexity of an internal model is proportionate to the materiality of a specific product or line of business. Limited scope of partial internal models may also be justified on the basis of transition to a full internal model or as a facilitation of specialization and innovation in a particular business area.

Having justified limited scope in terms of the undertaking's risk profile, materiality, stage of current progress, or proportionality, the challenge is to substantiate the technique by which these partial models will be integrated into the standard formula. CEIOPS will review any proposed technique against these criteria:

- Novelty of the technique and how extensively it has been used in common practice
- Its effectiveness in producing an accurately calibrated, risk-sensitive result
- Data requirements and need for expert judgment
- Whether quality academic and actuarial references exist

It is envisaged that the application process could have three possible outcomes, with first prize naturally being approval. Once approval is granted, the undertaking should begin using the model to calculate the SCR. In the case of a conditional approval, terms and conditions may first have to be met.

Limited approval may be offered by the regulator, which would mean that not all risk modules or business lines are granted internal models approval. In this case, the SCR for the remaining business lines would have to be calculated using the standard formula. Rejection would mean that an undertaking must submit a new application. The latter possibility cannot be taken lightly. Supervisors are well aware of the substantial number of large banks that have experienced successive failed Basel II implementations.

TESTS AND STANDARDS

The Level 1 text stipulates seven categories of tests and standards applicable to internal models. The most important of these is the use test, a concept borrowed from Basel II. The use test is a standard to which undertakings should adhere in the application of their models. There are also statistical standards, calibration standards, and ones for profit and loss attribution, validation, documentation, and external models and data.[6]

Given the importance of these tests and standards, CEIOPS has published all the requirements in a Level 2 implementation advice paper.[7] In fact, the substance of these tests and standards and their interaction becomes more clear through the Level 2 advice papers, as they create the context for models' desirable qualities in terms of their inputs and outputs and their role and function within the undertaking.

The first category of the stipulated tests and standards refers to the use test, which plays a pivotal role in the relationship an undertaking has with its supervisor. The undertaking must be able to demonstrate that the internal model is embedded within the day-to-day running and decision making of the business. The philosophy behind this principle is that the supervisor should have no reason to trust the model if the executives of the undertaking itself do not.

According to the use test, insurance and reinsurance entities should have only one modeling framework in place. This is necessary to ensure that the same model is applied to SCR calculation, internal decision making, and capital allocation. This model should be used to predict and discriminate risk, adjust risk appetite, set risk limits, measure performance and incentivize compensation accordingly, allow monitoring of large risk exposures, and produce risk management and risk reporting information, and it should be instrumental in the analysis of risk strategy, balance sheet optimization, and new products.

CEIOPS regards the use test as so important that it has developed a set of nine principles that supervisory authorities will use to assess compliance:[8]

Principle 1. Senior management and administrative management of an undertaking shall be able to demonstrate an understanding of the internal model. This includes the structure of the internal model, how it aligns to the business model, and the limitations of the model. With respect to the latter, management is required to understand the implications of market movements with respect to the company's portfolios, particularly when correlations break down. Senior management also must be able to develop a view on the consumption of regulatory capital as the ratio between eligible own funds and SCR changes over time.

Principle 2. The internal model must fit the business model. The alignment between the two should link to the technical provisions, reconcile internal and external reporting, including the functionality to review model output according to different accounting treatments, and be proportionate to the nature, scale, and complexity of the business. Any change in the business model should be reflected in the internal model. The proposed change policy should make allowances to reflect, for example, geographical or product line expansions or reorganizations.

Principle 3. The internal model should be used to support and verify decision making in the undertaking. The undertaking must be able to demonstrate that the internal model's results are in fact used in actuarial pricing, remuneration strategies, capital allocation, strategic decisions, and tactical decisions.

Principle 4. The internal model should take sufficient recognition of all the risks impinging on the business that are practically useful for risk management and decision making. In other words, the internal model has to be sufficiently material in respect to the risks that the undertaking faces that its output can be pertinent in decision making to the business in general.

Principle 5. The design of the internal model should facilitate analysis of business decisions. Model input and output should inform internal debate. Analysis of the future performance of the business or portfolio should be based on the same inputs and outputs. In other words, key business risk drivers should also be key model inputs if such a model is to be useful for decision making.

Principle 6. The internal model must be integrated with the risk management system. The internal model cannot be standalone; it has to be embedded within the architecture, processes, procedures, and policies of the undertaking. Integration is evidenced by risk rankings and risk quantification triggering action within the entity, among other things.

Principle 7. The internal model is to be used to improve the undertaking's risk management system. CEIOPS believes that undertakings will develop feedback loops that might improve risk mitigation techniques, clarify risk appetite, inform risk monitoring, and ultimately entrench more risk-based decision making.

Principle 8. An internal model should be integrated into the risk management system, as mandated by the previous two principles, on a consistent basis for all uses. Insurers cannot cherry-pick assumptions, valuation bases, accounting treatments, and calculation methodologies to create more "favorable" results on an ad hoc basis. In addition to any other reporting requirements that an undertaking may have, the risk management system and internal model shall include risk assessment and valuation of assets and liabilities on a Solvency II basis.

Principle 9. The SCR shall be calculated at least annually from a full run of the internal model. Recalculation is mandated if there is a material change in the undertaking's risk profile, if the assumptions underlying the model change, or if the methodology changes.

The second category of tests and standards mandated by the directive is that of statistical quality standards. Whereas the use test is more concerned with the purpose of the internal model, the goal of statistical quality tests is to ensure that the components of the internal model and its inputs pass quality standards. There are nine statistical quality standards. They cover:

1. Internal model and probability distribution forecast
2. Calculation methodology and assumptions
3. Data
4. Risk ranking and model coverage
5. Recognition of diversification effects
6. Recognition of risk mitigation
7. Financial guarantees and contractual options
8. Future management actions
9. Payments to policy holders and beneficiaries

In the first standard, CEIOPS refers specifically to a probability distribution forecast. Such distribution forecasts are generated by running numerous iterative scenarios through the models, based on the economic scenarios generated by the economic scenario generator (ESG). The results should be viewed as a series of probability distribution forecasts under various states of the world and whose results are then aggregated on the basis of a diversification method to create the SCR.[9]

The second standard mandates several requirements for the methodology employed in the calculation of the probability distribution forecast and the assumptions underlying the internal model. The methodologies should be "based on adequate, applicable, and relevant actuarial and statistical techniques," "consistent with the methods used to calculate technical provisions," "based upon current and credible information," and "based on realistic assumptions."

All assumptions must be identified, taking into account the significance and implications of the potential model error involved and the implications of alternative assumptions. What this means is that, for example, in making an assumption of an additional spread on a discount rate in the valuation of best estimate based on sovereign risk, the undertaking needs to state the assumption made, why the assumption has been made, and what the potential impact of the assumption would be in terms of model error.

The third standard refers to data. The data used in constructing the model are required to be "accurate, complete and appropriate." None of these terms is defined. Consequently, the undertaking must set its own standards in terms of its interpretation of these requirements. It must be able to justify to the supervisor why its data should be regarded as accurate, complete, and appropriate.

Interestingly, with regard to instances where expert judgment needs to be applied to data (e.g., when interpolating between points of a distribution or extrapolating to the tails of a distribution) CEIOPS clearly states that such expert judgment must be falsifiable, that it should be able to be proven false by experiment or observation. In addition, the expert is to make the uncertainty surrounding the decision transparent. All such judgments must be documented and validated.

This particular data quality standard is well worth remembering. When Basel II was first promulgated, no one had access to consistent haircut values for a wide range of collateral types, specifically those not traded in liquid markets. Initially no quantitative estimates were given for what these haircuts would be in the LGD calculations. Assumptions were therefore initially based on expert judgment. The criterion of falsifiability raises the bar substantially, in that such an assessment now has to be capable of being proved wrong, at least in theory.

Because an undertaking is required to set its own data standards, it must have its own data policy that specifies standards for data quality and a process to collect, update, and validate data. This implies that an undertaking requires a data governance policy.[10]

The fourth statistical quality standard requires that undertakings have the ability to demonstrate that the internal model is able to rank risk. That is, the entity must have the capability to discriminate between risk levels within a particular risk as well as across different types of risk. No particular absolute value or probability is necessarily assigned in a risk ranking system. What is important is that there should be sufficient risk categories to discriminate meaningfully between potential risk events or losses in a portfolio. It should also be demonstrated that the risk measure employed is the most suitable for that risk category, and that it is possible to scale or translate risk measures for the purposes of comparison across all risk categories.

According to the fifth area of statistical quality standards, undertakings determine their own risk categories for purposes of diversification. The system for measuring diversification benefits—in other words, for aggregating risk modules—must identify the key variables driving dependencies. This area should be seen as nontrivial. It is not simply the key variables driving individual risks that must be identified but the key drivers of the relationships between individual risks. These drivers can be estimated qualitatively, but the estimate must then be justified, and it has to be falsifiable.

Diversification benefits are not simply assumed to exist; their existence needs to be justified. The assumptions underlying the modeling of dependencies must also be justified. Joint distributions can be used relying on fairly straightforward mathematics by assuming that both underlying distributions are normal distributions, but if the underlying distributions are not normal, copulas or other more complex approaches must be used.[11] Extreme scenarios in the tail dependency need to be taken into consideration, which means that the tails of those distributions also need to be justified. If, for example, a nonempirical distribution is fitted to a series of data points, creating a theoretical distribution whose tails are too thin, fattening of the tails would have to be justified.

The robustness of the diversification system must be tested on a regular basis. Clearly, the diversification system may be prone to substantial change and transition over time if overfitted to key input variables. This means that an unstable model may produce vastly different results every quarter or every year. Undertakings should therefore have a system in place to regularly test robustness over time. A typical technique employed here is the construction of a transition matrix to assess the probability of risk exposures moving from one risk category to another within a particular risk type over a given period of time. Ideally, the cells around the diagonal of the transition matrix should have high values so that transition probability is low.

Risk mitigation techniques are the sixth area covered by the statistical quality standards. Conditions attached to full recognition of the risk-mitigating effects of reinsurance contracts, collateralized transactions, or any risk transfer instruments employed on the asset or liability side of the balance sheet are reasonably comprehensive in practice. Reflection of risk mitigants in the internal model must meet criteria such as the following:

- An economic effect must result through the action of risk transfer, regardless of legal form or accounting treatment.
- There should be legal certainty of enforceability.
- Liquidity requirements of mitigants must meet the requirements of the undertaking's own risk management policy.
- Secondary risks arising from the use of mitigants should be reflected in the internal model, including credit risk, concentration risk, basis risk, legal risk, operational risk, and model risk.
- Mitigants should be both irrevocable and unconditional.

The last three areas under statistical quality standards, covering financial guarantees and contractual options, future management actions, and payments to policyholders and beneficiaries, are concerned with the consistent recognition of uncertain future events in the internal model. Options and guarantees must be modeled consistently with the method used in the calculation of optionality in the technical provisions; expert judgment does not suffice for an accurate assessment. Any conditions beyond the control of the undertaking that will necessitate future management actions should be reflected in the internal model, such as the implications of strained market liquidity conditions or the need to change asset allocation strategy. All expected future payments to policyholders must be reflected, whether or not they are contractually guaranteed.

Having dealt with the use test and statistical quality standards, which can really be viewed almost as the rationale for, and skeleton of, internal models, the directive then articulates the required calibration standards under the third category of tests and standards.

According to the use test, undertakings should be able to use the output of their internal model for risk management and decision making. Because enterprises have different business models, the appropriate time period and risk measure used to model a capital requirement may differ widely. In this sense the standard Solvency II calibration of 99.5 percent over one year may be seen as quite arbitrary, but it is at least consistent across European insurers. Since the ultimate purpose of Solvency II is policyholder protection, the undertaking should be able to use a calibration most appropriate to its risk profile. The purpose of the calibration standard is thus to ensure an appropriate level of prudence in the SCR.

The majority of insurers are in fact substantially more prudent in their modeling than the standard calibration. It is not uncommon for solvency probabilities of up to 99.97 percent and time periods of 25 years to be used in value-at-risk (VaR) calculations. Additionally, given VaR's weakness in capturing the tail region beyond the loss number, many undertakings use the TailVaR measure.

Even so, a more conservative calibration does not exempt an insurer from any of the other tests and standards discussed here. An undertaking must be able to justify its choice of a time period other than one year on the basis of the duration of its liabilities and also must be able to demonstrate that its risks over one year are managed. To ensure "equivalent protection of policyholders" in the event that the SCR cannot be derived directly from the probability distribution as calibrated by the undertaking, it needs to rescale risks without introducing material bias and explain to the supervisor how it does so. It also has to explain any shortcuts that may have been used in the reconciliation of its internal model to the SCR.

Naturally, model calibration is a critical feature of model accuracy, to the extent that calibration may be susceptible to overfitting by modelers, or achieving results that are self-fulfilling. Calibration can also be dangerously inaccurate when model accuracy diminishes over time. Regular calibration is essential, particularly in cases where model accuracy has diminished over time. The ideal way for insurers to test this calibration internally is to run their calibrated portfolios against benchmarked portfolios on a regular basis and test them against external assumptions. If the supervisor has concerns regarding the calibration of the model, it may insist that the model is tested in this way.

Profit and loss attribution, the fourth category of the seven tests and standards, mandates undertakings to demonstrate that the sources and causes of profit and losses of each major business unit are reflected in the categorization of risk chosen in the internal model. CEIOPS points out that a sufficiently transparent profit and loss attribution method is intricately bound to the use test, as the results of profit and loss attribution provide the inputs not only to the undertaking's risk management function but also the system of governance more broadly, such as the own risk and self-assessment and capital allocation processes. To make this easier for undertakings to achieve in practice, CEIOPS advises using definitions for profits and losses that are consistent with the variable described by the probability distribution forecast. This definition may be basic own funds or something else used by the insurer for capital resource purposes, as long as the insurer is aware of how it differs from accounting profit and losses.

In addition to the use test, profit and loss attribution is also connected to the fifth category of tests and standards, stipulating the validation of the internal model. Because no model can predict the future with absolute certainty, even in the short term, not to mention over longer horizons, validation must be performed periodically to maintain confidence in the appropriateness of the model's underlying assumptions and specification. Backtesting is a common technique used in model validation.

The concept of backtesting as it applies to Solvency II is more comprehensive than the term is commonly understood in the context of banking.[12] For insurance undertakings, backtesting will include not only comparison of predictions with actual realizations, but also a comparison of predicted kernel calculation inputs against actual inputs as well as goodness-of-fit tests to probe the shape and stability of distributions.[13]

CEIOPS considers appropriate validation procedures as essential to the protection of policyholders. Since an "ideal" list of validation procedures is not feasible, given the wide variety of model types and risk profiles, supervisors will require undertakings to have a validation policy in place. This policy must cover:

- Purpose and scope of validation
- Validation tools
- Frequency with which model components will be validated
- Governance of validation results
- All known limitations of the validation policy
- Documentation of the validation policy
- Confirmation that the validation process is subject to independent review, including why the review should be considered independent

Although there is no ideal list of validation procedures, supervisors will demand that, at a minimum, the data, methods, assumptions, expert judgment, documentation, systems and information technology, model governance, and the use test itself shall be validated.

Category 6 of the tests and standards applies to documentation. Undertakings must comply with a long list of documentation requirements. Broadly, all aspects of the other categories of tests and standards must be comprehensively documented, to the extent that any conceivable, relevant component or area of the undertaking's internal model could be clarified to a third party thereby.

In terms of the seventh category of tests and standards, in the event that undertakings use external models or data in their internal models, they should be able to justify both the role played by external models and data and their preference for using them rather than internal data and models. The use of external models and data does not exempt undertakings from any of the precepts applicable to the other tests and standards.

CONCLUSION

What stands out in the regulations pertinent to internal models, and the expectations of the supervisors, is that the approval process and the tests and standards emphasize documentation, process control, the use test, and validation. These items require a very organized data and process framework and require that the entity has data governance in place.

A plethora of models exist within insurance entities. Actuaries often create models that reside on their laptops, but even where version control is in place, this tends to be quite disorganized and inconsistent across the insurer. Large insurers with large diversified portfolios in different geographical regions face an even greater challenge.

Experience from Basel II has taught that data governance is crucial to the success of any internal models program. In particular, if executives are to be able to meet the many stringent criteria, especially the use test, and demonstrate their familiarity with the working and performance of their internal model, a data governance strategy becomes essential.

CHAPTER **8**

People, Process, and Technology

KEY TO A SUCCESSFUL SOLVENCY II PROJECT

The Solvency II requirements contain a mixture of extremely complex quantitative calculations and risk management and governance processes, with a focus on auditability and transparency. Insurers will be required both to implement the necessary physical changes affecting how the business is run and to effect important cultural changes to ensure that Solvency II principles are embedded effectively into the business. To ensure success, insurers will need to consider the three critical components to a successful Solvency II project: people, process, and technology.

A potentially successful Solvency II implementation, or indeed any risk management project, generally requires integrating risk management as a key corporate initiative with a senior executive, typically a chief risk officer (CRO), responsible and accountable for the overall risk strategy of the insurance company. Having this organizational structure in place will facilitate the process of effectively defining and identifying the data sources and processes that are required before one can even begin assessing an insurance entity's optimal risk management strategy. The final part of the puzzle is determining the solutions and applications required to support an insurer's Solvency II and other risk management projects. Naturally, it is of paramount importance that these systems should be flexible enough to accommodate evolving risk and future data management requirements.

Stakeholders are increasingly, and understandably, strident in their demands for timely, accurate information; the onus is on the insurance company to provide the desired level of transparency within its risk management procedures. Certain insurers may consider a so-called best-of-breed approach to risk management. Although this approach may mitigate the problem in the short term, such a limiting approach typically fails to achieve even the required level of transparency when risk and data are aggregated at an enterprise level. In order to avoid the many potential pitfalls and resolve such issues, insurance companies are well advised to implement an end-to-end enterprise risk management solution.

PEOPLE

An organization's greatest resource and asset is without doubt its people. It is, of course, equally true that neglect of its resources could potentially prove ruinous to any organization.

A major business challenge facing many insurance companies today, including even certain relatively large, sophisticated players, is that they conduct business using a silo approach to managing information. Information is prepared at different frequencies, for different functions, and by different lines of business, making comparisons difficult or even impossible, with no way of easily or routinely aggregating risk data. In fact, many organizations struggle even to reconcile financial reporting with risk reporting where data have been aggregated in different ways in the same line of business. This problem arises because many organizations have not documented the data transformation processes for different functional requirements, such as standard financial reporting versus risk reporting.

Because insurers cannot aggregate the data, they are unable to gain an enterprise view of risk. There is no transparency of the risks at an enterprise level, and, generally, any formal focus on risk management is on the negative aspect of risk rather than taking a proactive approach to strategic risk management. This fragmented approach to risk—whereby, for example, the actuarial department is in charge of insurance or underwriting risk while investment officers are responsible for market risk—creates a false sense of security. Senior management may believe that the organization is managing risk, but, in fact, it may lack any insight into the common business situations where risk is manufactured. With this approach, insurers cannot really protect value or create value. The only real perspective offered is historical; businesses that are managed solely on a historical perspective cannot move forward in a way that creates value.

The Committee of European Insurance and Occupational Pensions Supervisors (CEIOPS) recommends that at least one executive, typically a CRO, be designated to oversee the risk management function; preferably a risk committee performs this function. Whether in the person of the CRO or a committee, the risk management function is also assigned ownership of the design and maintenance of the internal model(s). The appointment of a senior executive or risk professional to the CRO position has been widely adopted by the insurance industry. According to a 2010 report by the Economist Intelligence Unit (EIU),[1] over half (58 percent) of insurance companies had a CRO. Although certainly not an ideal situation, given that this function within many companies is still relatively new, it is perhaps not surprising that its authority level even now remains somewhat underdeveloped, particularly in relation to the other key C-level positions. For example, the reporting line of the CRO in most insurance companies is to the chief financial officer (CFO) and not the chief executive officer.

Even in an ideal world, simply appointing a CRO probably will not suffice. Large, sophisticated insurers in particular will need an enterprise risk committee with representation from all the business units. The purpose of this committee is to:

- Ensure a risk governance structure that allocates roles and responsibilities throughout the organization.

- Define the policies and procedures around risk identification, risk assessment, risk monitoring, and reporting.
- Comprehensively define risk objectives that articulate the institution's risk appetite.

Although it is the CRO's task to communicate its risk procedures and governance structures effectively throughout the organization, responsibility for the day-to-day management of risk rests with the business area where the risk was raised.

In addition to the ramifications of Solvency II for the various business units, consequences of its implementation will heavily impact the information technology (IT) department. Certainly one of the lessons learned from the recent financial crisis is that due to the complexity and potential severity of risk exposures underpinning the interdependence of risk management, a more advanced, integrated, and scalable infrastructure to protect insurers, policyholders, and other stakeholders in the future is required. The IT department will be responsible for providing the technology infrastructure that supports the Solvency II quantitative requirements and ensuring that the technology meets the auditability and transparency requirements. The IT capabilities that insurance companies should consider implementing for Solvency II compliance are discussed later in this chapter.

Implementing Solvency II within an insurer will be a major undertaking, irrespective of the organization's size. With many insurers actively recruiting for and embarking on major Solvency II projects, risk expertise is becoming a scarce, and expensive, commodity. According to a report in *Risk* magazine,[2] shortages of risk professionals in the United Kingdom are causing salaries to rise by 20 to 30 percent. Due to this potential scarcity of resources, insurance companies will probably hire external consultancy firms for expertise and advice. A Chartis Solvency II report[3] published in 2009 highlighted that the expenditure on professional services will grow at a healthy 14 percent compound annual rate. Initially this expenditure will be fueled by the demand for advisory services in risk modeling, risk governance processes, and methodologies. Then demand will shift from advisory work to actual implementation, including system integration, application configuration, and process management.

PROCESS

Solvency II requires not only that insurers meet capital requirements but that they can prove they have a sound and efficient risk management framework in place (i.e., the qualitative or Pillar 2 aspects of the Solvency II regulations). In fact, after the banking crisis, CEIOPS placed significant focus on the ability of insurers to demonstrate that they have embedded formal data and risk management processes within the organization.

From a risk management process point of view, it is extremely useful for insurers to have a deep and detailed documented understanding of their business and its processes. Doing this implies that insurers should gain a granular understanding of the sources of profitability and of risk against a range of critical business dimensions, such as region, customer type, product type, or line of business. In this way insurers are able to create risk versus return metrics that can be aggregated up to a group level from the most granular level. It is crucial that an insurance company be able to aggregate its risks from a granular level before it attempts to define its broad-based group-level strategy.

An efficient risk management framework should be organized around a circular process. This framework enables an insurer to define its risk appetite, evaluate and calculate risk taken, monitor the risk, and finally to take corrective action to reassess and adjust its risk appetite. There are six main components to a risk management framework:

1. Risk appetite
2. Risk evaluation
3. Data
4. Modeling
5. Aggregation
6. Reporting

For a risk management framework to be truly effective and to stand up to Solvency II regulatory scrutiny, it needs to establish well-defined risk objectives that articulate the insurer's risk appetite. The risk appetite is the amount of risk exposure or potential adverse impact from an event (or events) that the insurance company is willing to accept or retain. Once the risk appetite threshold has been breached, risk management treatment and business controls are implemented to bring the exposure level back within the accepted range.

For risk appetite to be properly understood, it must be evaluated clearly. One way of doing this is to implement automated monitoring of key risk indicators as soon as certain thresholds are reached, so that relevant risk information is constantly evaluated and managed. Once risk appetite and risk evaluation can be combined, one has access to a powerful mechanism not only for managing risk strategy but also more generally for enhancing overall business performance.

The raw material that feeds the Solvency II and risk management framework, and hence influences its results, is the quality and integrity of its data. Superior data quality, and consistent and complete data availability, is fundamental to the success of any risk strategy. Data quality deficiencies (that is, incomplete, inaccurate, missing, and/or out-of-date data) can seriously impede the successful implementation of any risk strategy or Solvency II framework. Organizations that have followed a typical silo-based approach, wherein disparate business units and multiple legacy systems have become embedded over time, will need to commit substantial effort to retrieve and consolidate the required data for Solvency II, test it, document it, and ensure that the process is auditable by both internal and external stakeholders.

Once insurers have consolidated the data by means of an enterprise risk data warehouse or other technological infrastructure, they can use the information to feed the sophisticated actuarial, capital modeling, and risk analytical tools to determine the valuation of assets and liabilities and to perform the complex Solvency II quantitative calculations.

Insurance companies often do a great job of assessing and evaluating risk at a granular level, such as the underwriting of a particular risk or quantifying default risk, but seldom view or understand the risk from a firm-wide level, taking into consideration interdependencies between risks. Historically, few business units report risk directly to the board of directors. This may change as regulators require more transparency and more board involvement. According to a 2009 report from the EIU,[4] nearly one-third (29 percent) of C-level executives highlighted developing a "firm-wide" approach to risk as a major initiative for their company. It is imperative to note that Solvency II explicitly requires a total balance sheet approach, meaning that insurance companies necessarily must aggregate underwriting risk, market risk, and credit and operational risk to calculate the solvency capital requirement (SCR). The total balance sheet principle is based on the notion that in order to manage risk properly, insurance companies need to build the capability of aggregating risks from different lines of business and across different risk types.

Risk reporting should be aligned to other strategic reporting initiatives to provide a clear view of risk performance and its consequences to the overall business. There is a clear value proposition here, as the reporting applications and business intelligence tools made possible by this alignment are also essential to disseminate relevant information to decision makers and to provide a clear set of risk versus return metrics. This granular and detailed risk reporting, aggregated to a group level, enables the organization to easily evaluate its risk appetite and take prompt corrective action as necessary.

The processes associated with a risk management framework are conceptually simple but can be difficult to implement in practice. The successful implementation is vitally important to all insurers, since the broadest consequence of Solvency II will be the pressure on companies to demonstrate that they have robust risk management processes in place.

TECHNOLOGY

Once an insurance company has created the appropriate risk team (people) and defined its risk management framework (processes), it can begin the task of defining its technology infrastructure and evaluating the technology capabilities required for Solvency II.

A Solvency II risk management framework would ideally include data integration, data quality management, enterprise risk analytics, and reporting capabilities in one seamless integrated solution. The aggregation of data from core systems into a single enterprise risk environment provides the foundation by which data and processes can be integrated into a production cycle that is repeatable and auditable.

Technology represents a significant proportion of the budget for any Solvency II implementation. According to the Chartis Solvency II technology report published in April 2010, the Solvency II software market will approach $1.7 billion by 2012.[5] Internal spend is expected to represent the lion's share of this amount, as insurance companies embed Solvency II processes and systems into day-to-day activities.

Data Management

As insurers embark on enterprise-wide risk management initiatives, a key challenge faced is that of data management. While it is well recognized that the integrity of internal data is very much the lifeline of insurance companies, there are significant challenges to aggregating data to create analytical metrics. The 2009 EIU report[6] highlighted the fact that the lack of data availability and data integrity is currently hampering the ability of financial services firms to implement enterprise-wide risk management capabilities. Nearly one-half of executives questioned (41 percent) in this survey considered improving data quality and data availability to be one of the three major areas of focus in the management of risk within their organization. The need for comprehensive data management infrastructure increases with the complexity of the risks and the size of the organization. In an EIU survey conducted in 2008,[7] it was reported that over one-half of the respondents (56 percent) agreed that it is essential to have an enterprise data warehouse in place.

Insurance companies can gain numerous insights from the challenges banks encountered implementing Basel II. Data management, not risk modeling, was perhaps one of the biggest issues banks faced. Banks that focused predominantly on risk modeling without consideration of the required data management capabilities, found that the repeatability and integrity of their processes were inadequate, leading to substantial variability in their reporting metrics. Models that had been built on manually extracted data suffered as a result of diminished data availability and reliability when run in production cycles. In cases where a silo-based approach for risk was followed, significant issues with the aggregation of data were encountered; portions of certain portfolios were ignored in the risk process while other portfolios were addressed by models with conflicting responses. Any insurer could well meet these same issues in organizations where risk models are built in silos and in environments that are not well suited to auditability. The use of incompatible data systems and processes increases the challenges faced by insurers in terms of discrepancies and inadequacies in the data.

Ideally, for successful Solvency II implementation, insurance companies would implement for the entire organization an enterprise data warehouse that would integrate all relevant information from internal IT systems and external sources and would serve as a uniform and reliable source for all necessary analytical tasks, including the calculation of solvency risk capital. In this way insurers can be sure that the same source data used for balance sheet reporting are also used for risk categorization codes. This is extremely important for the validity, transparency, and acceptance of analysis and reports.

It is convenient to view the successful implementation of the data management system as consisting of five core elements:

1. Defined data sources
2. Data exchange or ETL (extract, transform, and load) processes
3. Data quality
4. Unified data model and repository
5. Governance

A critical first step is to determine which of an insurer's numerous potential data sources will need data to be extracted in order to meet Solvency II requirements. The risk management technology infrastructure should be able to process and integrate information from a variety of sources, including front- and back-office applications. In certain cases, insurers face challenges—for example, expansion into new lines of business or previous mergers and acquisitions which have led to a multitude of legacy systems. These legacy systems, which cover functional areas such as policy administration, billing, claims, human resources, and counterparty ratings, often cause the proliferation of multiple data silos. In such cases, data will have to be extracted not only from numerous source systems but perhaps also from numerous downstream data silos. Nontraditional data sources now needed for Solvency II purposes, such as insurance company assets, market quotes for traded securities, and economic risk factors, will also have to be integrated into a single reliable source for all analytical processing.

Another challenge facing insurance companies has been the proliferation of a wide variety of data formats. Data may be stored in relational databases, flat files, outdated database formats, XML, or other formats. Additionally, some of the relevant data may be unstructured, free-form text.

Should the implementation of a data warehouse be considered, it is imperative to note that a data model should be used. The data model is a "single version of the truth" that stores comprehensive, accurate, consolidated, and historical information related to the insurance industry. It is an evolving entity that should be modified to reflect the changes that take place in the data elements themselves as a consequence of new business initiatives that will affect the enterprise risk management platform. According to Celent, "Insurers should consider purchasing a predefined data model, preferably one that is compatible with ACORD XML standards, from a systems integrator or technology vendor with deep experience in data mastery for insurance."[8]

A critical part of any data management project is for the organization to map source system data to an ideal data model from which all analytical processes will feed. This data mapping process and the construction of the ETL steps, including cleansing of data, is perhaps the most important challenge of any Solvency II implementation. It is generally recognized that 70 to 80 percent of the implementation effort for a risk management project is associated with data management. ETL tools, designed specifically for the insurance industry, can provide significant efficiencies and decrease implementation effort.

Data quality is paramount for any system that operates for the sole purpose of producing valuable business information. No insurance company can ever be sure that its economic and/or regulatory capital calculations are accurate and reliable if the supporting data are not cleansed and validated according to defined business rules. Techniques such as plots and descriptive statistics may be used to explore quality and integrity issues within data.

Consolidating data from different transactional systems, different product lines, and divergent geographies can expose data quality problems. In many cases, the level of data quality in source systems is unknown. Data warehouses or data marts created to support Solvency II and risk management in general will fall short if they are populated with questionable or low-quality data. Sources of poor data quality can include data entry errors, missing data, misapplied business rules, duplicate records, and out-of-range values.

For example, a simple description or abbreviation can result in multiple business meanings. Within auto insurance, the abbreviation "BI" stands for "bodily injury"; in business owner's policy insurance, "BI" means "business interruption." Another basic example of data inconsistency occurs if certain systems record vehicle details in a single field while others use three data fields: make, model, and year. These discrepancies are exaggerated as insurers attempt to implement cross-border data architecture.

The persistent occurrences of data quality issues throughout organizations, particularly in the financial services industry, have led to the burgeoning science of data governance. Data governance defines, for example, the role of a data steward, who takes responsibility for the reliability, availability, and utilization of data throughout the organization. Many organizations have instituted data governance officers and appointed data stewards and data owners in order to assign responsibility for the identified criteria to which data should adhere. The aggregation of data quality concerns through the implementation of a data governance framework allows organizations to address these issues at an enterprise level rather than as a business-as-usual concern in a silo-based approach. A vital component of any risk management system is the ability to reproduce the results from a regulatory and governance perspective. To do this, insurance organizations need to keep the underlying data that were used to create the results reported to external stakeholders, including regulators.

To address this requirement, data infrastructure is critical. This infrastructure must at a minimum be able to generate audit trails and trace the source of information and results throughout the life cycle of data, from the point of extraction to report generation. This ability will allow regulators and internal auditors to validate the results produced by the risk management process on a regular and ongoing basis. The implication of this validation requirement is that insurers will need to implement data management infrastructure that maintains historical data at a granular level, allowing for back-testing, historical simulations, and the comparison of calculations and analyses between multiple time frames.

Risk Analysis

A significant portion of the Solvency II framework is dedicated to the quantitative requirements for European insurance companies. Organizations that continue using silo-based risk management at a spreadsheet level will not meet these requirements easily. Difficulties in aggregation and auditability, as well as dependence on key personnel performing manual tasks within spreadsheets, will seriously hamper the ability to comply with Solvency II requirements.

Actuarial, risk calculation, and capital modeling tools will be needed to help insurers calculate and aggregate risks. Such tools also will be used to determine the minimum capital requirement and solvency capital requirement. In addition, these risk analytical tools need to support stress testing and scenario simulation.

The EIU 2009 survey[9] noted that over one-quarter (27 percent) of financial services executives consider better and more sophisticated analytics as a key focus area. Insurance companies will need an end-to-end technology infrastructure that is scalable with sufficient processing power to support the increased complexity and sophistication required for Solvency II calculations.

Reporting

Solvency II not only demands huge amounts of extra reporting from insurance companies produced in shorter time periods; it also demands that these reports be more rigorously controlled and documented. Insurers will need a mechanism to distribute these reports to all business departments, including senior management, as well as external parties in a timely manner.

Business intelligence and reporting applications are essential to provide reporting capabilities and dashboards for decision makers. These reporting tools should include report templates for the supervisory (Pillar 3) requirements such as the Solvency and Financial Condition Report and the Report to Supervisor.

In addition, the reporting software should be flexible enough to allow users to generate tailor-made reports and consolidated reporting at different levels and risk types. For example, a risk dashboard should be customizable for different users, such as the CFO, CRO, and actuaries. The system should allow the presentation of a clear view of the risk status, using key risk indicators at all levels of the organization, integrating risk data from market, underwriting, operational, and credit counterparty risk.

CONCLUSION

Implementing a Solvency II project will be a major undertaking for an insurance company, irrespective of its size. Critically, organizations should view this implementation process as cutting across all departments and divisions and necessarily requiring people, processes, and technology enhancements. The fundamental basis of any successful implementation will be reliance on high-quality data, to ensure that Solvency II reports are viewed as having complete integrity. The need for data integrity and data quality calls for a significant investment in understanding the granular data processes required to aggregate risks and financial metrics to an enterprise level. Both CEIOPS and national regulators have stressed the importance of the integrity and quality of data in the production of the solvency capital requirements.

CHAPTER 9

Business Benefits

REGULATION PAST AND PRESENT

Regulations may be regarded by business owners and business managers as an additional cost of doing business, having a drag effect on the speed with which the organization can innovate as well as tending to drag on the organization's profitability. From a business manager's perspective, excessive regulation can appear to micromanage the entity's operations and limit its strategic potential. From a business owner's perspective, the concern might be more aligned to the earnings per share (EPS) impact of significantly costly or onerous regulation.

In many private enterprise undertakings, regulation is limited to employee safety, product safety, and, particularly in industries with high barriers to entry, limiting anticompetitive practices. Certain industries, however, are subject to significant regulation, notably those with parastatal characteristics or those engaged in the provision of utilities. The tension that has existed over the past century or more between the concept of the free market and the necessity to protect the individual has led in certain industries, particularly finance, to a fascinating mix of free market economy concepts embedded in a regulatory framework of rules-based and principles-based regulation.

A very good example, as witnessed over the past decade, has been the instance of the Basel II Accord implementation, containing a multitude of rules, regulations, classifications, and limitations on banking, coupled with the simultaneous emergence of increased complexity and innovation in the financial sector. It is ironic that this period of time, which saw the introduction of a detailed set of banking regulations that are precise and limiting in many ways, has also seen the proliferation of financial innovation, at least some of which has proven deleterious to the health of the financial sector and the real economy more broadly. These financial innovations have correctly been blamed to a large extent for the failure of the banking system over the past several years and have demonstrated a degree of greed and a general lack of foresight that perhaps reveal an underlying need for regulation within the financial services industry in general.

Since the Basel II Accord was scripted during the same period of time in which these instruments took hold within the economy, there have been significant criticisms levied against the Accord. However, it has been quite correctly pointed out that the Basel II stipulation was implemented in the European economies only after the causes of the financial crisis had already been firmly rooted. In fact, the Basel II Accord came too late to temper the extent of these financial innovations. Although Basel II may have proven somewhat shortsighted in certain areas, many other factors were also at work, such as the external credit assessment institutions and global imbalances in sustaining what in hindsight proved to be overly loose monetary policy.

Bankers have responded somewhat cynically to the significant increase in regulations going forward as well as to the vitriolic tone accompanying the proposed new regulations. In light of these facts, a fundamentally important question is: What value should be accrued in one's planning for Solvency II? This is not as simple a question as one would have expected a decade ago, when the concepts underlying Basel II—for example, the concept of economic capital—were being proposed as a capital saving remedy and an efficiency gain to those organizations willing to accept the costs of implementation and advance to the more sophisticated internal ratings–based approach.

The prevailing mantra of proponents of the economic capital approach was that economic capital would allow improved dynamic capital allocation. This would allow banks to run a thinner capital base, owing to increased awareness and understanding of risks within their respective organizations. The determination of business benefit thus seemed quite simple and easy to sell, as the benefits could be calculated as the opportunity costs of capital, owing to a reduction in capital requirement, under the assumption of a move away from the simple risk weights of the standardized approach toward the more advanced internal ratings–based approach. In fact, most banks today are aware of the significant reputational advantages of holding excess capital, of not running a thin capital base, and of being able to boast that their sources of funding are more stable and less aligned with capital markets than those of their competitors.

The concept of capital allocation nowadays is seen as beneficial more in terms of seeking risk-adjusted efficiency within one's own organization than in comparison to one's competitors. It is perhaps a misnomer in today's post–financial crisis world to view the Basel II or Solvency II regulations as being substantially beneficial purely on the basis of capital efficiency. In fact, the real business benefit to a full-scale implementation of the Solvency II regulations would be far more enduring than any annualized capital efficiency metric.

Successfully implementing a Solvency II regime within an organization necessitates considerable understanding on the part of both executives and line managers of the risks inherent to all portfolios, on both the asset and the liability side of the balance sheet. During the implementation of Basel II at numerous banks, for example, it became clear that the real issue lay not in the implementation of an economic capital calculation but more in the gathering, storing, and management of data and information in a sufficiently robust form to allow the necessary calculation to take place in the first place.

Given the enormous size of insurance companies today, having to apply a set of regulatory rules in a consistent manner across all portfolios and aggregate positions in a nonlinear fashion using a series of economic assumptions to create a distribution of possible scenarios necessitates an enormous effort in collecting, storing, and reporting data and information throughout the organization. In many cases these exercises have never before been performed, as they have not previously been required by any regulation or internal strategy.

It has been argued that certain jurisdictions have already formed almost all of the necessary functions embedded in Solvency II, although this is certainly not necessarily true. In fact, the consistency required under the Solvency II regime in the typology and classification of risk types or risk modules does not necessarily exist within many organizations. Nor is there necessarily consistency in the manner in which risk modules are aggregated. Actuarial practice and actuarial assumptions have been relatively consistent across portfolios of liabilities, but the Solvency II regime will encourage and perhaps force large and medium-size insurance groups to be completely consistent in their classifications and typology of risk modules as well as in their approach to measuring these risks, across both asset and liability sides of the balance sheet.

BENEFITS OF AN ENTERPRISE DATA MANAGEMENT FRAMEWORK

Potential benefits of an enterprise data management framework far outweigh the benefits of mere consistency of risk classifications and application of regulation. The lifeline of any system that is designed to derive valuable business benefit and draw pertinent conclusions from processed data is the data themselves. With constant performance pressures and Solvency II demands, insurance companies are being forced to collect more data and dig deeper into their databases to refine their analyses. In fact, CEIOPS has enforced the importance of data quality, which in the committee's experience is a major area of concern for European insurers.[1] CEIOPS expects insurance companies to:

- Have a data dictionary of all data sources and attributes.
- Conduct data quality assessments.
- Take steps to remediate any identified issues.
- Demonstrate that ongoing data quality monitoring processes are in place.

CEIOPS also stresses the need for expert judgment to validate any objective data quality measures, adjustments approximations, and use of historical data.

Data management is an essential component of a Solvency II solution. An insurer's approach to data management should be holistic and unified, as data silos stymie the flow of information and prevent employees and managers from seeing a complete picture of the organization's risk exposure and overall business. An insurance company's data management framework must:

- Be scalable
- Be open
- Be capable of supporting the needs of multiple risk management functions and business applications
- Provide analytical capabilities, such as stress testing, and solvency capital requirement and minimum capital requirement calculations
- Be able to produce reports for a variety of internal and external parties

The structure of that data is of critical importance to the viability of a Solvency II solution. The most significant issue that banks faced in implementing the Basel II Accord was data, not modeling. The banks found that the data required were not available in a consistent or reliable form to populate their growing range of models. Today many banks emerging from Basel II are citing much improved data quality as one of the key business benefits. Hence, from a change management perspective, insurance companies should start early to design a data management framework that is flexible enough to support Solvency II and anticipate future risk management requirements. As covered in Chapter 8, integration is likely to be the most costly part of any Solvency II project. Choosing the right enterprise technology in which to build the data extraction tools, workflows, reporting templates, and other enterprise features is a key step.

Data management and data quality are no longer optional components of a regulatory solution; they are essential. Solvency II's more sophisticated approach to risk management, financial reporting, and corporate governance requires insurance companies to put comprehensive standards, policies, and processes in place for the use, development, and management of data. The legislation calls for data relating to risk to be generated more frequently and more thoroughly to support the new processes. Firms will need to demonstrate that they have instilled risk awareness and sensitivity in all core activities.

Insurance companies are continuously trying to make better business decisions faster. However, many insurers spend so much time manually gathering and cleaning data and creating reports that there is little time left to explore data for insights that can have a positive impact on the bottom line. That is why a holistic, unified approach to data management, which ensures a smooth flow of information throughout the organization, is a critical part of a true risk management system. This approach will enable decision makers to glean key insights from the data and then combine those with insights from other business functions, such as marketing, claims, and underwriting. The benefits of cross-functional insights are ultimately realized in true enterprise-wide risk-based performance management, business intelligence, and management information systems.

BENEFITS OF AN ECONOMIC BALANCE SHEET

This data-driven approach accrues significant benefit to any organization. The consistency that is necessitated by the regulations will result in uniformity across reporting, analysis, and predictive capability in those organizations that properly implement the Solvency II regulations at a granular level. It will furthermore create the capacity for improved strategic planning, performance management, and remuneration strategies that add value to the organization on a risk-adjusted basis. In many cases, it will allow organizations to identify portfolios that are less than optimal in their performance and to focus on building portfolios that are more advantageous to the long-term sustainability of the insurance entity. From the perspective of the organization, it will also embed the creation and maintenance of corporate history, in the process removing significant key-man risk and dependence on the islands of data and information ownership that continue to plague large organizations.

The alignment under the economic balance sheet approach also implies a far greater recognition of risk at a more granular level and an ability to align risk-based reporting standards with accounting-based reporting standards. Performance attribution, allocation of resources, internal efficiency, strategic planning capability, and overall operational management would significantly improve in an organization that has made the effort to collect all necessary underlying data for Solvency II purposes in a single, managed, consistent data-driven environment.

It has been demonstrated time and time again that the real benefits that accrued to bank managers in their implementations of the Basel II Accord were ones that had far more to do with understanding internal portfolios than with immediate capital reduction benefits.

From a shareholder perspective, Solvency II would provide far greater granularity and transparency across all portfolios and across all sources of risk than at any time previously. One thinks for example of AIG and how the risks inherent in its massive credit default swaps (CDS) positions would have been identified and reported under a Solvency II regime. A total economic balance sheet approach would have necessitated a marking to market of the CDS position at AIG. The financial products division is believed to have written around $1 trillion of such protection, notwithstanding the fact that this sum far exceeded the capital available to pay claims. AIG's models incorrectly assumed low default correlation rates between assets underlying collateralized debt obligations, seemingly generating large alpha returns for the financial products division, until of course the bubble burst.

Although Solvency II implementation costs may shave a few cents off earnings per share, this should be balanced by the benefit of a far more transparent, and consistently transparent, set of reporting requirements than before. The nature of the economic balance sheet, and the manner in which it captures risks on both the asset and liability sides of the balance sheet, results in a holistic view in which the natural interplay between risky assets and liabilities can be identified. This is a substantial improvement on the Basel II requirements, which mainly focus on the asset side of the balance sheet.

BENEFITS IN PERSPECTIVE

The real purpose of Solvency II is the protection of policyholders. The benefits of the proposed regime are clear. Solvency II's supervisory ladder of intervention approach would have been useful for banks during the financial crisis and will ensure far greater protection for policyholders than previously, owing to the early-warning and early-response nature of the Solvency II Directive. The regulations force consistency in terms of the classification of risk, the granularity at which that classification takes place, and the measurement of risk, albeit on a principles-based versus rules-based approach. This valuable information will lead to improved economic planning, insight, and the ability of insurance entities to embed their own early-warning mechanisms. Such a regime would have resulted in red flags being raised on AIG far earlier than was the case, owing to AIG's significant concentration in the CDS asset class. On a comparative basis, the information gathered by regulators through the Solvency II reporting process will allow them to observe distortions on either the asset, liability, or both sides as well as to elicit distortions on a jurisdiction basis between countries.

The business benefits of implementation that large insurance companies cite in justifying the significant costs of implementation go beyond mere regulatory approval, and include strategic, operational, and governance aspects.

Forward-looking strategic planning will be aided by the improved capital allocation and performance evaluation as a result of the information made available by Solvency II processes. The balance sheet capital structure will be founded on a more risk-based approach, rather than a purely returns-based approach, which is more advantageous for capital management. Improved group strategic management is enabled by a far better understanding of the interplay between risk and return within and between portfolios. This understanding facilitates better, more appropriate, forward-looking decisions in terms of product sets, remuneration strategies, and client sectors to which to market.

Increased transparency will aid external parties as well; for example, improving the ability of ratings agencies to assess both overall industry and individual capital adequacy. Group reporting standards should help to contain reputational risk, improve transparency, and bridge the gap between accounting standards and risk-based reporting.

However, the really significant benefits lie in operational efficiency resulting from the construction of a granular corporate memory, which is necessitated by the level of detail that Solvency II regulations demand.

BENEFITS BEYOND SOLVENCY II

The insurance industry has already traveled some way down the improved risk management road. Firms have had varying degrees of success in implementing risk standards, but there is certainly much still to be done. Solvency II will continue this drive and provide further impetus for the development of a component firm-wide risk management framework that is integrated into the industry governance and business decision-making process.

Insurance executives must make a declarative choice in developing the Solvency II business case. A firm can elect to do the minimum required to implement the legislative change to ensure compliance, which is less expensive in the short term but is bound to entrench a disadvantage over the long term, as it implies a higher cost of capital and results in less sophisticated risk management capabilities. Or firms can invest in enterprise technology and integrate risk management into their core business processes to achieve competitive advantage and, as a result, maximize potential benefits.

By investing in an enterprise risk management solution, insurance companies can optimize the use of Solvency II resources and turn the compliance burden into a number of strategic opportunities. A number of recent examples, most notably AIG and Equitable Life, have highlighted the damage and loss of trust in management that inadequate risk management can cause. Hence, relevant and accurate disclosure of risk and capital management can improve confidence and restore reputation.

In addition, insurance companies can use the Solvency II regulations to build a brand that is recognized for its strength of capital position, transparency in its operations, and sound risk management practices. The benefits of such a brand are apparent in increased market share and retention of existing customers.

Rating agencies are encouraging insurers to manage risk and capital in a way that enhances the quality of earnings. According to rating agency AM Best, an insurer that can demonstrate strong risk management practices integrated into its core operating processes, and effectively execute its business plan, will maintain favorable ratings in an increasingly dynamic operating environment.

It should also be mentioned that an effective risk strategy would have to contain, or be accompanied by, a reinsurance strategy to reduce the insurer's risk levels. Reinsurance optimization applications integrated into the risk management framework can calculate and determine which kinds of risks an insurance company wants to cede. Such an application can also be used to assess which and how many reinsurers will act as counterparties, how the reinsurance contracts will be designed, and what implications reinsurance has for risk and return on capital.

Solvency II is considered an exceptionally ambitious project, the objectives of which have been designed to generate benefits to both policyholders and insurance companies. However, if the directive is executed properly and the anticipated benefits are realized, it could have a dramatic impact on the European economy. The new framework will apply uniformly across the European Union, helping to speed the arrival of a true single market in financial services. In addition, more efficient capital allocation, coupled with greater transparency and improved public reporting, will almost certainly lower the risk of company failure, ultimately leading to greater confidence in the industry and bolstering financial stability. The improved financial strength of the larger European insurers will inevitably provide them with the resources to expand into both mature and emerging overseas markets.

CONCLUSION

This book has endeavored to emphasize that an enthusiastic embrace of the Solvency II framework by industry executives, and support for its implementation, is a positive step toward developing a holistic picture of the organization's risk exposures, risk appetite, and ongoing strategic evaluation of its business model. In terms of regulations, it will become incumbent on executives to communicate an understanding of their own risk exposures, risk management and governance processes, and risk models to external stakeholders.

The regulation of industry has in the recent past been regarded as an unnecessary hindrance to the dynamism of economies and the natural tendency of firms to innovate and expand. Since the 2008 financial crisis, public sentiment has turned against the financial sector's view of how it should be regulated and even against the preferences of regulators themselves.

As the eurozone debt crisis unfolded in early 2010, Berlin unilaterally banned naked short selling. Germany's finance minister, Wolfgang Schäuble, justified the move saying: "If you want to drain a swamp, you don't ask the frogs for an objective assessment of the situation."[2] At the time Angela Merkel conceded that the decision may be technically inadvisable but nevertheless was politically appropriate. Given the enormity of the financial sector bailout and the consequent ballooning of public debt in many countries, it may be a long time before we return to a more normal state of the world in which debt levels are manageable and wherein the voting public is not suspicious of regulations presumed to be laissez-faire. As a result, financial services firms globally face significant regulatory uncertainty for many years, perhaps decades, to come.

Seen in this light, Solvency II may be regarded as a timely regulatory framework. Chapter 6 described in some detail how the total balance sheet approach creates the foundation for a principles-based regulatory framework with the ultimate objective of policyholder protection. The articulation of this objective by CEIOPS and ratification by the European Parliament removes, to a large extent, the possibility of arbitrary prescriptions on, or political meddling in, the business models of insurers down the road, their capital requirements, risk management processes, or governance structures.

Moreover, there has been continuous involvement over a number of years by the industry itself in the formulation of the directive. Given the substantial input made by the insurance industry, the regulations may be seen as a reflection of the principles by which insurers themselves believe they should be regulated. On the downside, concerns have been raised in certain quarters that the standard formula will subject smaller insurers to unreasonable capital requirements, but it seems unlikely that the European Commission will allow the industry to remain hobbled in this way. The framework allows insurers considerable discretion in building and implementing internal models, as long as data and model validation and statistical quality rules are adhered to.

All insurance firms have in common the provision of products that offer consumers the ability to mitigate against an uncertain future, and are therefore critical to economic stability. Application of the Solvency II principles should create the necessary conditions to establish the credibility of the European insurance industry in the minds of consumers into the foreseeable future.

By taking an early and proactive stance toward the implementation of Solvency II, individual insurers can achieve the sustained benefits of competitive advantage through improved business intelligence and management information systems.

In addition, it must be recognized that in a political climate of significant distrust of corporate entities, the implementation and endorsement of a principles-based regulatory framework presents a strikingly superior alternative to being subject to ham-fisted and heavy-handed regulation.

Notes

Chapter 1

1. In the first known elucidation of the tragedy of the commons, Aristotle notes in *Politics*, circa 350 BC, that private property is desirable from a social welfare point of view: "that which is common to the greatest number has the least care bestowed upon it. Everyone thinks chiefly of his own, hardly at all of the common interest; and then only when he is himself concerned as an individual."

2. Council of the European Parliament, "Directive of the European Parliament and of the Council on the Taking-Up and Pursuit of the Business of Insurance and Reinsurance (Solvency II) (Recast)" 2009, available online at: http://register.consilium.europa.eu/pdf/en/09/st03/st03643-re06.en09.pdf.

3. The sixth Babylonian king Hammurabi (ruled ca. 1796–1750 BC) codified the mores and customs of the day in the Code of Hammurabi. The preface to the code states: "Anu and Bel called by name me, Hammurabi, the exalted prince, who feared God, to bring about the rule of righteousness in the land."

4. Thirteenth-century traders of these Italian maritime states were the first Europeans to use double-entry bookkeeping. The mathematician Leonardo Fibonacci (ca. 1170–1250) introduced the Hindu-Arabic concept of zero to Italian bookkeepers through his book the *Liber Abaci* (Book of Calculation), allowing profit margin and interest calculations.

5. Joint stock ventures as practiced by Genoese and Venetian merchants should not be confused with the very much later invention of joint stock companies.

6. The mathematician Pierre-Simon Laplace remarked in *Théorie Analytique des Probabilités* (Analytic Theory of Probabilities) (1812):

"It is remarkable that a science which began with the consideration of games of chance should have become the most important object of human knowledge."

7. In 1693, Edmund Halley created the first mortality tables, but it was not until 1762 that a viable business model for life insurance became possible, when the Equitable Society for Assurance of Life and Survivorship introduced mortality tables into its premium calculations to vary premiums based on the age of the insured.

Chapter 2

1. The University of Chicago economist Frank H. Knight was the first academic to formally present this distinction between risk and uncertainty: "a measurable uncertainty, or 'risk' proper . . . is so far different from an unmeasurable one that it is not in effect an uncertainty at all." John Maynard Keynes was later to elaborate on this theme in *The General Theory of Employment, Interest, and Money* (1936), wherein he coined the now universally recognized term "animal spirits," which he characterized as: "not . . . the outcome of a weighted average of quantitative benefits multiplied by quantitative probabilities." Clearly Keynes viewed the behavior of markets as driven substantially by forces that cannot be captured quantitatively, in effect by uncertainty, which in today's world we refer to as risk. More recently there has been a shift in thinking, in that these animal spirits which rule our behavior can perhaps be tamed. Tversky and Kahneman's *Prospect Theory* (1979) recognizes that behavior can to some extent be modeled. Their pseudocertainty effect demonstrates people's natural tendency to misevaluate the likelihood of events with both extremely small and extremely high probability, depending on their psychological framing. This explains why, for example, an individual may buy both a lottery ticket and an insurance policy without experiencing any dissonance in terms of their sense of relative risk aversion. Prospect Theory and more recent behavioral economics demonstrate that individuals are in general incapable of quantifying uncertainty, or in other words assessing risk. Well-developed insurance markets assist individuals in evaluating and pricing risks

in both their personal and professional lives with which their mental accounting is simply not wired to cope.

2. Insurer Solvency Assessment Working Party of the International Actuarial Association, "A Global Framework for Insurer Solvency Assessment" 2004, available at: www.actuaries.org/LIBRARY/papers/global_framework_insurer_solvency_assessment-public.pdf.

3. As far back as 1980 Sanford Grossman and Joseph Stiglitz pointed out a paradox. If security prices reflect all information, no gain accrues from going to the trouble of collecting it. More recently the behavioral economist Richard Thaler has characterized the efficient markets hypothesis as consisting of a "price is right" component and a "no free lunch" component. The market crisis of 2008 would seem to have falsified "the price is right" component by falsifying the rational expectations hypothesis that people do not make systematic errors in their expectations of the future. At the same time the market crisis has provided strong evidence for the "no free lunch" component, since risks are often more correlated than they seem and high returns based on leverage may be illusory.

4. Insurers distinguish between the term *peril*, the cause of a loss, and *hazard*, a circumstance or condition that increases the probability of a loss occurring.

5. Simple, standardized contracts are traded on the Chicago Board of Trade and the Chicago Mercantile Exchange. Standardization makes these derivatives transparent, while the position of the clearinghouse as counterparty renders them effectively default free. The vast majority of derivatives are, however, not exchange traded but rather bilateral contracts traded over the counter, such as those mentioned in the text. The Bank for International Settlements estimates the total notional value of all outstanding interest rate derivative contracts at December 2008 as $418.7 trillion.

6. The need to fund liabilities via growth in risky assets can hold the potential for disaster if insurers are unable to hedge or derisk balance sheets as appropriate through the economic cycle. The International Monetary Fund mentions four factors that eroded

insurers' solvency buffers as the banking and credit crisis of 2008 unfolded: (1) procyclicality of solvency, accounting, and valuation requirements; (2) diversification benefits reduced as asset correlations tended to 1; (3) lower interest rates increased the net present value of liabilities; and (4) asset price volatility increased the costs of policy guarantees. The procyclicality of existing solvency regulations and monetary policy, the existence of model risk, and the behavioral aspects underlying the volatility of asset prices were known before the crisis, but were not necessarily properly factored into insurance models.

7. These default probabilities are according to Standard & Poor's average transition rate matrix for corporate debt over 1981 to 2004. Moody's and Fitch are the other two big recognized rating agencies.

8. A general property correction will also manifest in weaker performance of mortgage-backed debt issues. The monoline insurance companies offer protection against credit default of issuers, allowing lower-rated issuers to issue highly rated bonds by providing a backup guarantee in exchange for a premium. In 2007, as the U.S. housing market crashed, losses began to soar on the insurance of structured credit products backed by residential mortgages. The eventual downgrading of Ambac Financial Group by Fitch to AA in early 2008 triggered the simultaneous downgrade of over 100,000 bonds. Bloomberg, "Ambac's Insurance Unit Cut to AA from AAA by Fitch Ratings" (January 19, 2008), available at: www.bloomberg.com/apps/news?pid=newsarchive&sid=asLtTQyLRQQs&refer=home.

9. Berkshire Hathaway Inc., "2002 Annual Report" p. 15, available at: www.berkshirehathaway.com/2002ar/2002ar.pdf.

Chapter 3

1. As reported in "Why Insurance Companies Fail," a working party report under the chairmanship of Roger Massey delivered at the 2002 General Insurance Research Organizing (GIRO) Committee convention.

2. The European Commission began its review of the European insurance industry, Solvency II, in May 2001. The Working Group of insurance supervisors was asked to make recommendations to the commission based on an analysis of any trends that could be identified in the risks confronting insurers. The report, compiled between June 2001 and December 2002, is known as the Sharma Report after chairman Paul Sharma of the United Kingdom's Financial Services Authority.

3. Hurricane Betsy was the first to cause over $1 billion of damage ($1.4 billion in unadjusted 1965 dollars). St Helen's Insurance was placed into run-off in 1989, due in part to those earlier losses but also through the impact of unforeseen losses on long-tail liability insurance from asbestos claims in the 1980s.

Chapter 4

1. Structured credit products and their acronyms have proliferated over the past two decades. Collateralized loan obligations (CLOs), collateralized bond obligations (CBOs), mortgage-backed securities (MBSs), and asset-backed commercial paper (ABCP), stand as examples.

2. "Citigroup Chief Stays Bullish on Buy-Outs," *Financial Times* (July 9, 2007).

3. This metaphor has recently been popularized by the applied statistician, trader, and author Nassim Taleb, whose books demonstrate the inadequacy of Gaussian distributions used in statistical modeling in the face of catastrophic events.

4. The Black-Scholes model for pricing options in continuous time came into widespread use after a 1973 paper by Robert Merton enhanced previous work by Fisher Black and Myron Scholes. The crucial assumption underpinning the model is that the underlying stock price follows a lognormal or continuously compounded probability distribution of returns as it evolves through time. The model's central insight is that an option has an implicit price as long as the stock is traded. Merton and Scholes were recognized for their work with a Nobel Prize in 1997.

5. The Senior Supervisors' Group is composed of senior supervisors from seven supervisory agencies: the French Banking Commission, the German Federal Financial Supervisory Authority, the Swiss Federal Banking Commission, the U.K. Financial Services Authority, and, in the United States, the Office of the Comptroller of the Currency, the Securities and Exchange Commission, and the Federal Reserve.

6. This section draws heavily on the Senior Supervisors' Group report. Although the report covers the period to end 2007, its general findings are equally relevant to conditions experienced through 2008 and indeed any crisis.

Chapter 5

1. " 'Solvency II': EU to Take Global Lead in Insurance Regulation," European Union Press Release, July 10, 2007, available at: http://europa.eu/rapid/pressReleasesAction.do?reference=IP/07/1060.

2. Run-off usually refers to insolvent insurers. These insurance companies are no longer accepting new business, but continue to process existing business. In the case of life insurance companies, they may be in run-off for many years.

3. Moody's, "Solvency II for European insurers: No Widespread Rating Actions Expected, but Major Improvements to Companies' Risk Management" (June 18, 2006).

4. International Association of Insurance Supervisors, "Guidance Paper on the Use of Internal Models for Risk and Capital Management Purposes by Insurers" (October 2007), available at: www.iaisweb .org/__temp/15__Guidance_paper_No__2_2_6_on_the_use_of_ Internal_Models_for_regulatory_capital_purposes.pdf.

5. Article 102 of the directive in fact states that the SCR should be calculated annually. However, since MCR and supporting own funds are required to be calculated quarterly, by implication so is the SCR. CEIOPS has noted that a quarterly recalculation of the SCR would be quite burdensome in practice. As implemented, quarterly recalculation of the SCR will probably be on the basis of a "carryforward" of the previous SCR, perhaps as a percentage of technical provisions.

6. CEIOPS, "Advice for Level 2 Implementing Measures on Solvency II: Supervisory Reporting and Public Disclosure Requirements," (October 2009).
7. CEIOPS, "Draft Advice to the European Commission in the Framework of the Solvency II Project on Pillar II Capital Add-ons for Solo and Group Undertakings," (November 2006).
8. CEA, "Solvency II Main Results of CEA's Impact Assessment" (June 2007), available at: www.cea.eu/uploads/DocumentsLibrary/documents/Solvency%20II%20Impact%20Assessment%20FINAL.pdf.
9. "Solvency II QIS3 issues," *The Actuary* (November 1, 2007), available at: www.the-actuary.org.uk/698030.

Chapter 6

1. Mark to market means a complete departure from the world of book value accounting. In book value accounting, instruments and assets are depreciated through their lifetimes on the balance sheet and the depreciation is written to the income statement. Mark to market is an attempt to calculate the economic value of an instrument at a point in time, primarily based on the theory of net present value of future cash flows, netted between payments in and payments out on a swap, for example. This departure from book value accounting in the field of market risk management for the trading book of banks' balance sheets became inculcated within the accounting field under the international accounting standards (IAS) 39 rules.

2. Credit default swaps permit speculation on changes in CDS spreads of single-name obligors, as an example. If one believes that a company is about to default, one can speculate on the entity's perceived credit quality deterioration through buying or selling CDS protection against default. An investor buying such protection is referred to as being short the CDS and the underlying bond. After Lehman was allowed to fail, trust evaporated from the short-term funding markets, leaving market participants in a state of catatonic fear, signaled by extreme gyrations in CDS spreads. Iceland's three largest banks, Glitnir, Kaupthing,

and Landsbankinn, experienced spreads on their bonds of nearly 1,000 basis points in September 2008 just prior to failure.

3. At J.P. Morgan's 1993 annual research conference, VaR was demonstrated to institutional clients, generating such interest that many asked to buy or lease the system. Till Guldimann, leader of the team that developed VaR, proposed that the firm make the system freely available so clients could implement it themselves. A service called RiskMetrics was developed comprising a technical document detailing the underlying computational assumptions and methodology as well as the necessary covariance matrix, updated daily and distributed free of charge over the Internet from October 1994.

4. The most popular analytical parametric method used during the implementation of VaR has been the variance-covariance method or so-called delta-normal approach, which was initially created by J.P. Morgan.

5. In a much-cited paper, Artzner, Delbaen, Eber, and Heath (1999) demonstrate that a measure purporting to satisfy the criteria for establishing the amount of regulatory capital that an entity requires to make its risk acceptable to the regulator (in an idealized sense) must have certain properties. Only a risk measure that satisfies all these conditions is said to be a coherent measure of risk: (1) monotonicity, (2) translation invariance, (3) homogeneity, and (4) subadditivity. VaR always satisfies the first three properties, but portfolios can be constructed in such a way that the fourth principle is violated.

6. CEIOPS, "Advice for Level 2 Implementing Measures on Solvency II: Valuation of Assets and 'Other Liabilities'" (October 2009).

7. QIS4 is segmented into 16 lines of life insurance business, differentiated according to contract type and risk drivers; separate health insurance contracts with features similar to life insurance; 12 non-life insurance lines of business; proportional non-life reinsurance treated as direct insurance and nonproportional reinsurance segmented into 3 business lines.

8. Articles 100 through 127 of the Level 1 text stipulate the requirements for calculating the SCR. There is a subsection relating to the general stipulations, another for the requirements

for calculating the SCR according to the standard formula, and a third for the requirements when adopting the full or partial internal models approach.

9. A matrix of correlation coefficients is stipulated for the aggregation of the risk modules; it can be found in Annex IV of the directive.

10. Solvency I capital requirements on insurance type liabilities are based on simplistic formulae, disregarding the actual risk profile of the business.

11. Harry Markowitz demonstrated in a 1952 paper, "Portfolio Selection," that rational investors select investment portfolios based on the parameters of return (mean) and risk (portfolio variance). A trade-off between risk and return is considered, which he named the efficient frontier, such that portfolio diversification using assets with a low or negative correlation allows investors to optimize risk for a given return and vice versa. William Sharpe and John Lintner advanced the portfolio approach to risk management in the mid-1960s with the introduction of the Capital Asset Pricing Model (CAPM). The CAPM shows that the risk of an individual asset can be decomposed into a diversifiable or idiosyncratic risk component and a nondiversifiable or systematic risk component. As a result, in a market that prices assets efficiently, the price (expected return) of an asset reflects the relative risk contribution, beta (β) or systematic risk of that asset, to the risk of the market portfolio. Markowitz's key insight was that diversification optimizes risk per unit of return or optimizes return per unit of risk, thus solving the problem of how to measure risk on a portfolio of different assets, as opposed to simply adding stand-alone risk per asset together.

12. In 1900, Louis Bachelier used the concept of geometric Brownian motion to model stock options in his PhD thesis, "The Theory of Speculation," but never received the recognition he deserved during his lifetime. Brownian motion as applied in finance derives from physics equations describing the diffusion of heat. The idea is that asset prices follow a "random walk" from an "equilibrium" price. Only five years later Einstein derived the partial differential heat/diffusion equation describing the motion of electrons in his

paper on Brownian motion, apparently unaware of Bachelier's work. A full 73 years before Black-Scholes, Bachelier derived the price of an option by working out the distribution, now known as the Wiener stochastic process, and linking it with Fourier's diffusion equation, to capture "drift." The method is crucial to financial mathematics as it allows one to derive a series of values at a future date, creating a frequency distribution that is assumed to be normal, and hence providing a closed form solution for the pricing of options.

Chapter 7

1. Taking its theoretical cue from Merton's contingent claims hypothesis, Basel II's basic premise with respect to the measurement of portfolio credit risk is that uncertainty in the world can be encapsulated into a single input, known as the asymptotic single risk factor approach (ASRF). The ASRF allows diversification benefits between assets to be captured by assuming that all obligors' credit risks are exposed to the same systematic risk factor, interpreted as the general state of the economy, while obligor-specific risks cancel out in infinitely granular portfolios.

2. ESGs produce economic scenarios for risk factors to be used by the asset and liability models for market consistent valuation purposes in an iterative way. Multiple valuations of both sides of the balance sheet are generated based on the values produced for each risk factor per iteration, in order to create a frequency distribution for the calculation of SCR. This can be done on a risk submodule as well as on a total balance sheet basis. Underlying risk factors of an economic scenario generator should be based on individual risk factor parameters that can be calibrated through statistical and econometric methods.

3. The requirements are stipulated in Articles 101, and 112 to 116 of the Solvency II Directive.

4. The principle of proportionality is invoked so that requirements imposed on small and medium-size insurance and reinsurance entities, and the level of supervision to which they are subject, are not too onerous. The directive recognizes that specializing in

particular customer segments and risk types can itself be a valuable tool for managing risk. Specific mention is made of captive insurers in this regard. In terms of the proportionality principle, provision is also made for undertakings to be allowed to use their own data in the calibration of the underwriting risk modules in the standard formula SCR.

5. An undertaking is an insurance or reinsurance entity that has made application for approval.

6. Article 120 makes provision for the "use test," a standard to which undertakings should adhere in the application of their models. Statistical standards, of which there are nine areas or subcategories, are articulated in Article 121. Calibration standards are laid down in Article 122. Articles 123 through 126 respectively specify standards for profit and loss attribution, validation, documentation, and external models and data.

7. These are found in CEIOPS' Level 2 advice paper, "Articles 120 to 126 Tests and Standards for Internal Model Approval."

8. Ibid.

9. ESGs are by no means exempt from the stipulations of the use test or those relating to external models. Executives will have to understand how the particular ESG implemented in their undertaking works.

10. Data governance is an evolving discipline that many large organizations are beginning to employ as the framework for exercising proactive control over data quality, data management, business process management, and risk management processes. A typical data governance structure defines the roles and responsibilities associated with data throughout its life cycle, so that data can be formally managed as a corporate asset.

11. Establishing accurate correlations between the chosen variables is of utmost importance. In cases where the underlying risk factors are not normally distributed, the use of copula functions may be required. Simply put, a copula is a multivariate joint distribution defined on the n-dimensional unit cube $[0, 1]n$, where every marginal distribution is distributed uniformly over the interval $[0, 1]$. Sklar's theorem for copulas underlies most of the applications. The theorem states that given a joint distribution function

H for *p* variables, and respective marginal distribution functions *Fi*, there exists a copula *C* such that the copula binds the margins to give the joint distribution.

12. Insurers will however employ techniques similar to those used in banks. Given the common problem of limited data, insurers will use various time horizons. Backtesting becomes more rigorous the shorter the holding period. To resolve the issue of an unrealistic holding period assumption, banks usually scale up their 1-day VaR to a 10-day VaR using the square root of time rule. By multiplying the daily VaR by the square root of 10, a 10-day VaR may be approximated, based on the assumption that the portfolio is equally risky daily and that daily returns are independent. The choice of confidence interval also has implications for the backtesting process. Whereas a confidence level of 99.97 percent may be employed to achieve, for example, an AA rating, in the backtesting context, a lower confidence level may be desired so that a more reasonable number of VaR spikes can be observed and tested against. Backtesting a model at, say, 96 percent, which implies an incidence of roughly 10 VaR spikes a year, may also have the advantage of increasing transparency in limit-setting processes and by implication more disciplined adherence to limit policies.

13. A model may backtest accurately, even perfectly, over a period of years before failing, potentially catastrophically. No statistical model can pretend to comprehensively and consistently capture the risk of correlated events of the magnitude sometimes experienced under abnormal markets. Empirically, financial markets are not "normal." Many financial returns time series exhibit severe leptokurtosis, or fat tails. The statistical assumption of the independence of events does not hold in markets during turmoil, since risk in markets is then driven by feedback effects. For example, the requirement for firms listed on the NYSE to report quarterly partly explains the rapid decline in prices of collateralized debt obligations, as the requirement for mark-to-market pricing drove observed prices down in an illiquid market.

As a result, it is essential to perform nonstatistical stress tests as an adjunct to VaR modeling, since models are built under assumptions that may not hold under certain scenarios. Whereas VaR is capable of estimating a distribution of probable future outcomes reasonably well, stress tests are a desirable complement to this baseline probabilistic scenario. Stress tests can be categorized broadly as being either sensitivity or scenario tests. Sensitivity tests apply arbitrary magnitude shocks to specific risk factors as a first approximation to the impact on portfolio value of a market move: for example, a 200 basis point increase in the short-term interest rate or a 30 percent exchange rate depreciation. More complete scenario tests impose a plausible configuration of risk factors on the baseline scenarios, corresponding to a hypothesized market event of particular significance to the specific portfolio or, more commonly, actual historical scenarios such as the Asian financial crisis of 1997. Furthermore, scenario tests often involve first order and second order effects, where analysts are required to understand the impact on the portfolio of second-round effects that result out of the initial shocks.

Chapter 8

1. Economist Intelligence Unit, "Rebuilding Trust: Next Steps for Risk Management in Financial Services" (April 2010).
2. "Risk Recruitment Shifts to Former Front-Office Execs," *Risk* magazine (December 2009).
3. Chartis Research, "Market for Solvency II Technology" (April 2010).
4. Economist Intelligence Unit, "After the Storm: A New Era for Risk Management in Financial Services" (June 2009).
5. Chartis Research, "Market for Solvency II Technology."
6. Economist Intelligence Unit, "After the Storm."
7. Economist Intelligence Unit, "The Bigger Picture—Enterprise Risk Management in Financial Services Organizations" (September 2008).
8. Celent, "Insurance Data Mastery Strategies" (November 2008).
9. Economist Intelligence Unit, "After the Storm."

Chapter 9

1. CEIOPS, CP43 "Technical Provisions—Standards for Data Quality," 2009.
2. "Upstarts Are Ill-Placed to Shake Up British Banking," *Financial Times* (May 21, 2010).

Glossary

Adjustment for the risk-absorbing properties of future profit sharing
Adjustment to the summation of the basic solvency capital requirement (BSCR) to reflect the potential mitigation of unexpected losses through a simultaneous decrease in technical provisions and deferred taxes provided by insurance contracts with discretionary future benefits.

Alternative risk transfer
Transfer of insurance risk by means of securitization, such as, for example, catastrophe and longevity bonds, or the transfer of certain risks from an insurer by means of reinsurance.

Arm's-length transaction
A related party transaction conducted so as to preclude any conflicts of interest.

Asset-liability management
The International association of Insurance Supervisors (IAIS) defines asset-liability management as "the management of an insurer's assets with specific reference to the characteristics of its liabilities so as to optimize the balance between risk and return."

Available own funds
The capital resources available to support the SCR, equal to the market-consistent valuation of assets less the market-consistent valuation of liabilities.

Backtesting
Comparison of actual experience against statistical predictions.

Bancassurance
Holdings in banks by insurers or vice versa to sell insurance and funds management products through bank sales channels.

Basic solvency capital requirement (BSCR)
The capital requirement reflecting the aggregation of underwriting risks, market risk, and default risk, before the addition of the capital requirement for operational risk and the adjustment for the loss absorbing capacity of technical provisions to give the solvency capital requirement (SCR).

Best estimate
Probability-weighted average of the expected value of discounted insurance liability cash flows. The best estimate and the risk margin add up to the technical provisions.

Biometric risk
Underwriting risks associated with the life status of a policyholder, for example, life expectancy, disability, marital status, and number of dependents.

Catastrophe risk
A low-frequency, high-impact event, or series of events, leading to significantly higher claims volumes than estimated.

Concentration risk
Exposure to losses through inadequately diversified portfolios of assets or liabilities. Such concentrations may occur in exposures to individual counterparties, a related group of individual counterparties, geographic locations, industry sectors, and catastrophes or natural disasters.

Confidence level
Probabilistic expression of the level of certainty of an outcome. It is usually expressed as the probability value $(1 - \alpha)$ in a percentage associated with a specified confidence interval, for example, the confidence level associated with a risk of ruin of one in two hundred years, $\alpha = 0.005$, is equal to 99.5 percent.

Cost of capital approach
Approximation used to determine the risk margin needed to cover the capital requirements of insurance liabilities in transfer to a third party. The approach determines the cost of capital to the third party of the capital required to support the liabilities.

Credit risk
The risk of a change in the value of assets due to actual credit losses greater than expected credit losses as a result of counterparties' failure to honor their obligations.

Default risk
The risk of possible losses due to unexpected default, or deterioration in the ratings of, debtors or counterparties over the following 12 months.

Disability risk
The risk of a deviation from the estimated rate of insured persons rendered incapable of fully performing the duties of their occupation.

Diversification benefits
Reflect the reduction in total institutional risk through the aggregation of uncorrelated asset and liability risks. In other words, the sum of the whole is less than the sum of the parts.

Economic balance sheet
A balance sheet comprised of market-consistent values for both assets and liabilities. Synonymous with the total balance sheet approach and solvency balance sheet.

Eligible own funds
Capital instruments that an insurer may take into account in determining the available funds for solvency purposes.

Embedded option
The right granted to a policyholder by an insurer to exercise a particular choice with respect to an insurance obligation.

Equity risk
The risk of loss as a result of a deviation in the actual value of the return on equities from their expected value.

Exit value
Amount the undertaking would have to pay to another entity to transfer all contractual rights and obligations. This is the market-consistent value of the insurer's portfolio.

Expected loss
In credit risk, the European Union's Capital Requirements Directive defines expected loss as "the ratio of the amount expected to be lost on an exposure from a potential default of a counterparty or dilution over a one year period to the amount outstanding at default." Expected loss may also be thought of as the probability of loss upon which a basic premium rate or interest rate is calculated.

Expense risk
The risk of a deviation in actual expenses associated with the servicing of insurance contracts from those estimated.

Fair value
The amount for which an asset could be exchanged or a liability settled, between knowledgeable, willing parties in an arm's-length transaction.

Foreign exchange (FX) risk
The risk of a deviation in actual exchange rates from those expected when liabilities and supporting assets or capital are denominated in different currencies.

Free capital
Amount by which available own funds exceed the solvency capital requirement. Synonymous with surplus capital.

Going-concern basis
Assessment of the financial situation of an entity under the assumption that it will continue to operate.

Guarantee
Payment or benefit to which a policyholder is entitled. Alternatively, a contractual assurance of the fulfillment of an obligation by a counterparty of higher credit standing.

Health insurance
According to the Committee of European Insurance and Occupational Pensions, "Health insurance obligations are all types of insurance compensating or reimbursing losses (e.g., loss of income) caused by illness, accident or disability (income insurance), or medical expenses due to illness, accident or disability, whether preventive or curative (medical insurance)."

Hedgeable risk
An asset or liability risk that can be neutralized by buying or selling a market instrument.

Insurance obligation
The balance sheet liability associated with honoring an insurance contract. Synonymous with insurance liability and best estimate.

Interest rate risk
The risk of an exposure to losses on financial instruments as a result of fluctuations in interest rates.

Internal model
According to the International Actuarial Association, a "mathematical model of an insurer's operations to analyze its overall risk position, to quantify risks and determine the capital to meet those risks."

Lapse risk
The risk of losses as a result of unanticipated policy lapse rates, including policy lapses, terminations, or surrenders. Losses are realized through the payment of termination or surrender values, and the inability to recoup initial policy acquisition costs via future premiums.

Life insurance
Insurance contracts whose benefits are contingent on the occurrence of death or disability, or life status of the insured at maturity of the contract. Contracts may take the form either of life or death coverage of an individual, paying either of a lump sum or annuity to a beneficiary.

Life risk
The risk of loss as a result of the level, trend, and volatility of mortality risk, longevity risk, disability risk, life expense risk, revision rate risk, the level and volatility of policy lapse rates, and the occurrence of extreme or irregular events (life catastrophe risk) deviating from those that are expected.

Liquidity risk
The risk of not being able to meet funding requirements at assumed rates, or the risk of an asset not achieving its expected value because of a lack of marketability.

Longevity risk
The risk of loss in a life insurance portfolio as a result of actual mortality rates being lower than expected.

Loss given default
The loss on an exposure as a percentage of the amount outstanding at default.

Market-consistent valuation (MCV)
Valuation of assets and liabilities by mark-to-market or mark-to-model techniques to reflect economic value rather than accounting value.

Market discipline
Mechanism for imposing discipline on undertakings by the transparency and credibility established through public disclosure of financial and risk information.

Market risk
The risk of a change in value of financial instruments as a result of market values deviating from those expected. Market risk is comprised of foreign exchange risk, property risk, interest rate risk, equity risk, spread risk, and concentration risk.

Market value
The amount for which an asset could be exchanged or a liability settled, between knowledgeable, willing parties in an arm's-length transaction. This is similar to fair value but for the fact that fair value may rely on mark-to-model techniques where no actual market price exists.

Market value margin (MVM)
The deviation risk of liability cash flows approximated by the present value of the cost of capital to cover the solvency capital requirement of the liability in run-off. Synonymous with risk margin.

Mark-to-market valuation
The valuation of assets and liabilities using current market prices.

Mark-to-model valuation
The valuation of assets and liabilities by modeling of market-consistent parameters.

Minimum capital requirement (MCR)
The lowest threshold on the supervisory ladder of intervention triggering supervisory measures. The regulator will likely place an undertaking whose available funds drop below this threshold in run-off, or transfer its liabilities to a third party.

Model risk
The risk that the model chosen deviates significantly from reality due to misspecification of the model or inappropriate model choice.

Morbidity risk
The risk of losses in a life insurance portfolio due to actual disability and illness rates of policyholders deviating from those expected.

Mortality risk
The risk of losses in a life insurance portfolio due to actual mortality rates being higher than expected.

Non-life insurance
Generic term denoting all types of insurance that are not life insurance. Non-life insurance contracts are usually short-term, and are variously known as general insurance or property and casualty insurance.

Non-life risk
The risk of loss in a non-life insurance portfolio as a result of fluctuations in the timing, frequency, and severity of insured events (premium risk), in the timing and amount of claim settlements (claims risk), and the occurrence of extreme or exceptional events (catastrophe risk).

Parameter uncertainty risk
The risk of loss in an insurance portfolio due to uncertainty in the estimation of parameter values applied in a model.

Premium risk
The risk of loss in a non-life insurance portfolio due to claim sizes, the timing of claims payments, and the frequency of claims deviating from those expected.

Probability of default
The probability that a counterparty will not honor its contractual obligations. The term is applicable to both debtors and reinsurers.

Probability of ruin
The probability that total net cash outflows will at any time exceed available resources over a given time horizon.

Procyclicality
The cumulative pressure on financial institutions to sell assets or raise capital at the same time, thereby exacerbating extreme market movements.

Property risk
The risk of loss as a result of the value of properties held deviating from those expected.

Prudent person approach
The requirement to act in the way that a prudent person would, for example, by considering risks, obtaining and acting on appropriate professional advice, and suitably diversifying investments.

Reinsurance
Risk mitigation in respect of insurance liabilities on the basis of an insurance contract between a reinsurer and insurer to indemnify against losses, whether partially or fully, in exchange for a premium.

Reserve risk
The risk of loss in a non-life insurance portfolio due to the size, timing, and frequency of incurred claims deviating from those expected.

Revision risk
The risk of loss in a life insurance portfolio due to unanticipated adjustments to annuity cash flows.

Risk margin
The deviation risk of liability cash flows approximated by the present value of the cost of capital to cover the solvency capital requirement of liabilities in run-off. Synonymous with market value margin.

Run-off
An insurer in run-off continues to operate on a going concern basis, but is precluded from writing new business, continuing to operate until the end of the term of insurance contracts underwritten by it.

Solvency capital requirement
The capital required to be held by an insurer to meet the Solvency II Pillar 1 capital requirement.

Spread risk
The risk of loss in a portfolio of assets due to the actual price of credit risk deviating from that which is expected.

Standard formula
The set of calculations prescribed by the Solvency II Directive and the Committee of European Insurance Supervisors to calculate the solvency capital requirement for insurers not implementing internal models.

Stress test
A solvency assessment that considers the impact on the combined asset and liability values of an insurer under a defined set of adverse scenarios.

Supervisory ladder
The scale of control levels at which capital levels trigger supervisory measures. The lowest threshold is the minimum capital requirement (MCR) and the highest the solvency capital requirement (SCR).

Supervisory review process
The process under which a supervisor evaluates whether an insurer fulfills the regulatory requirements.

Surplus capital
Amount by which available own funds exceed the solvency capital requirement. Synonymous with free capital.

Systematic risk
Risk that cannot be mitigated by diversification as it is market wide. Antonym of idiosyncratic risk.

Technical provision
The probability-weighted average of the expected value of all discounted cash flows associated with an insurance liability.

Total balance sheet approach
A balance sheet comprised of market-consistent values for both assets and liabilities. Synonymous with the economic balance sheet and solvency balance sheet.

Underwriting risk
The risk of loss in an insurance portfolio due to actual claims payments deviating from those expected. Comprised of life risk, non-life risk, and health risk.

Unexpected losses
In credit risk, unexpected losses are the difference between the maximum loss incurred and the expected loss at a specific confidence interval. In underwriting risk, unexpected losses occur when claims exceed expected levels.

Value at risk (VaR)
A measure of the potential loss on a portfolio of assets or on the total balance sheet. VaR estimates the worst loss expected at a given confidence level over a specified horizon.

Workers' compensation insurance

Insurance cover for work-related medical care or rehabilitation as a result of injury at work, on the way to or from work, and work-related diseases. Compensation may extend to wage loss and disability or death benefits.

Selected References

Chapter 1

Costello, D. "Recent Developments in Insurance Insolvency," 2003, available online at: www.actuaries.ie/Events%20and%20Papers/Events%202003/2003-02-12_Current %20issues/2003-02-12_Insurance_Insolvency.pdf.

de Roover, F. "Early Examples of Marine Insurance," *Journal of Economic History* (November 1945).

Diacon, S., C. O'Brien, and A. Blake. "The Economic Value of General Insurance," Association of British Insurers, 2005.

Dickson, P. G. M. *The Sun Insurance Office 1710–1960*. Oxford, U.K.: Oxford University Press, 1960.

Trennery, C. F. *The Origin and Early History of Insurance Including the Contract of Bottomry*. London: P. S. King and Son, 1926.

Vaughan, E., and T. Vaughan. *Fundamentals of Risk and Insurance*. Hoboken, NJ: John Wiley & Sons, 2008.

Chapter 2

Arrow, K. J. "Uncertainty and the Welfare Economics of Medical Care," *American Economic Review* 53, no. 5 (1963).

Arrow, K. J. *Essays in the Theory of Risk-Bearing*. Amsterdam: North-Holland Publishing, 1971.

Comité Européen des Assurances, Groupe Consultatif. "Solvency Glossary" (2007); available online at: www.cea.org.

Filipovic, D., and D. Rost, on behalf of the Chief Risk Officer Forum. "Benchmarking Study of Internal Models" (2005); available online at: www.croforum.org.

Insurance Solvency Assessment Working Party. *A Global Framework for Insurer Solvency Assessment*. International Actuarial Association, 2004.

International Monetary Fund. "Global Financial Stability Report" (April 2009); available online at: www.imf.org/external/pubs/ft/gfsr/2009/01/pdf/text.pdf.

Keynes, J. M. *The General Theory of Employment, Interest, and Money*. London: Macmillan, 1936.

Knight, F. H. *Risk, Uncertainty, and Profit*. Boston: Houghton Mifflin, 1921; available online at: www.econlib.org/library/Knight/knRUP.html.

Risk Management Working Party. "Liquidity Risk in Life Insurance" (2005); available online at: www.the-actuary.org.uk/697752.

Swiss Re. "Natural Catastrophes and Man-Made Disasters in 2008: North America and Asia Suffer Heavy Losses" Sigma (no. 2, 2009).

Chapter 3

Betz, S. "The Swiss Solvency Test for Non-Life Insurance," Actuarial Review (2006); available online at: www.casact.org/newsletter/pdfUpload/ar/CAS_AR_Aug2006_1 .pdf.

CEA. "Solvency II, Understanding the Process" (2007); available online at: www .cea.eu.

CEIOPS. "Quantitative Impact Studies Results" (various); available online at: www .ceiops.org.

CEIOPS. "Solvency II—Final Advice on Level 2 Implementing" (various); available online at: www.ceiops.org.

CEIOPS. "Submissions to the EC" (various years); available online at: www.ceiops.org.

Council of the European Parliament. "Directive of the European Parliament and of the Council on the Taking Up and Pursuit of the Business of Insurance and Reinsurance (Solvency Ii) (Recast)" (2009); available online at: http://register.consilium.europa .eu/pdf/en/09/st03/st03643-re06.en09.pdf.

European Commission. "The Application of the Lamfalussy Process to EU Securities Market Legislation" (2004); available online at: http://ec.europa.eu/internal_market/ securities/docs/lamfalussy/sec-2004-1459_en.pdf.

FSA. "ICAS—Lessons Learned and Looking Ahead to Solvency II" (2007); available online at: www.fsa.gov.uk/pubs/other/icas_isb.pdf.

FSA. "Solvency II: A New Framework for Prudential Regulations of Insurance in the EU" (2006); available online at: www.hm-treasury.gov.uk/d/solvencyII_ discussionpaper.pdf.

Insurance Solvency Assessment Working Party. *A Global Framework for Insurer Solvency Assessment*. International Actuarial Association, 2004.

Jorgensen, P. "Traffic Light Options," Social Science Research Network, 2006.

Massey, R. (chairman), et al. "Insurance Company Failure," Working Party Report to the General Insurance Convention, 2002.

Sharma, P. (chairman), et al. "Report: Prudential Supervision of Insurance Undertakings." Conference of the Insurance Supervisory Services of the Member States of the European Union, 2002.

Chapter 4

Basel Committee on Banking Supervision. "International Convergence of Capital Measurement and Capital Standards" (July 1988); available at: www.BIS.org.

Basel Committee on Banking Supervision. "International Convergence of Capital Measurement and Capital Standards" (June 2006); available at: www.BIS.org.

"Briefing: Modern Finance," *The Economist*, October 18, 2008.

International Association of Insurance Supervisors. "Guidance Paper on the Use of Internal Models for Risk and Capital Management Purposes by Insurers" (October 2007); available at: www.iaisweb.org.

Senior Supervisors' Group. "Observations on Risk Management Practices during the Recent Market Turbulence" (March 2008).

Chapter 5

CEA. "Amended Proposal for the Solvency II Directive" (2009), available online at www.cea.eu.

CEA. "Results and Discussion on the Impact Assessment of the Future Solvency II Framework on Insurance Products and Markets" (March 2007).

CEIOPS, Consultation Papers 17, 33, 37, 57, 58, (2008), available online at: www.ceiops.org.

Financial Services Authority. "Insurance Risk Management: The Path to Solvency II" (September 2008), Discussion Paper 08/4.

IAIS, "Use of Internal Models for Risk and Capital Management Purposes" (October 2007).

Kumar, N., and P. ChandraShekhar. "Understanding Solvency II," *InfoRm* (November 2005).

PriceWaterhouseCoopers. "Gearing Up for Solvency II: Making Solvency II Work for the Business" (2007), available online at: www.pwc.com/gx/en/insurance/solvency-ii/pdf/pwc_gearing_up_for_sovency_ii_0908.pdf.

Chapter 6

Artzner, P., F. Delbaen, J. Eber, and D. Heath. "Coherent Measures of Risk," *Mathematical Finance* 9, no. 3 (1999): 203–228.

Black, F., and M. Scholes, "The Pricing of Options and Corporate Liabilities," *Journal of Political Economy* 81 (1973).

CEIOPS. "Advice for Level 2 Implementing Measures on Solvency II" (2009); available at: www.ceiops.org.

Comité Européen des Assurances. "Why Excessive Capital Requirements Harm Consumers, Insurers and the Economy" (2010); available online at: www.cea.eu.

CRO Forum. "Calibration Principles for the Solvency II Standard Formula" (2009a), available at: www.croforum.org.

CRO Forum. "Internal Model Myths" (2009b); available at: www.croforum.org.

German Insurance Association. "Key Positions on Own Funds under Solvency II" (2007); available at www.gdv.de.

Lintner, J. "Security Prices, Risk and Maximal Gains from Diversification," *Journal of Finance* 20 (1965).

Markowitz, H. "Portfolio Selection," *Journal of Finance* 7 (1952).

Merton, R. "Theory of Rational Option Pricing," *Bell Journal of Economics and Management Science* 4, no. 1 (1973).

Nocera, J. "Risk (Mis)Management," *New York Times Magazine*, January 4, 2009.

RiskMetrics. *Technical Document*, 4th ed. JP Morgan/Reuters, 1996.

Sharpe, W. "Capital Asset Prices: A Theory of Market Equilibrium under Conditions of Risk," *Journal of Finance* 19 (1964).

Chapter 7

Artzner, P., F. Delbaen, J. Eber, and D. Heath. "Coherent Measures of Risk," *Mathematical Finance* 9, no 3 (1997): 203–228.

CEIOPS. "Articles 120 to 126: Tests and Standards for Internal Model Approval," 2003.

About the Authors

David Buckham is the founder and president of Monocle Solutions, an international risk assessment and optimization company that provides various products and consulting services by way of intellectual property. Since the creation of Monocle Solutions, David has worked on numerous corporate and institutional risk management and performance management projects, from both strategic and quantitative perspectives. He has delivered lectures and seminars on credit and market risk principles, and delivers training and consulting in areas ranging from credit scoring to structured financial modeling. David has a Bachelor of Science in Mathematics and an MA in Literature from the University of Cape Town.

Jason Wahl is head of research at Monocle Solutions. Since joining Monocle Solutions, Jason has worked on diverse risk management implementations at both European and South African financial institutions. His interests include the regulation of financial institutions, financial stability, and the applicability of risk modeling. Jason has a master's degree in Economics from the University of Stellenbosch.

Stuart Rose is global insurance marketing manager at SAS Institute, a market-leading business intelligence and analytics software vendor. Stuart began his career as an actuary and now has over 20 years of experience in the insurance industry. Prior to working for SAS, Stuart worked for a leading global insurance company in its life-and-property and casualty divisions as well as for a variety of software vendors, where he was responsible for marketing, product management, and application development. He has been responsible for the successful development and implementation of enterprise systems working with insurance companies in the United States, the United Kingdom, Europe, and South Africa. Stuart graduated from Sheffield University with a BSc in Mathematical Studies.

Index